EDITORIAL

PATRICK M^cGUINNESS

I first encountered *Poetry Review* in 1987, in the British Council library in Bucharest, a creaking prefab in the grounds of the British Embassy. To get into the compound, you had to show your papers to the ostentatiously-armed state militia. The locals endured random refusals, long waits, demands for non-existent or unproduceable documentation, and other types of casual sadism perpetrated by the badly-off upon the even-worse-off. There was also the certainty that, for every handful of locals allowed in, there was also an informer or two, reporting back on what they read, who they spoke to or on the kinds of material available in this strange British enclave in the centre of a police state.

One of the items a Securitate informer might have come across was the Autumn 1987 issue of *Poetry Review*. It was the first I read, and featured an article by an Irish poet about East European poetry in translation. I had a flash of dislocated recognition, because one of the poets reviewed was Marin Sorescu, the great, bleak, droll and self-effacing Romanian poet I had heard read and met twice in my time in Bucharest. Sorescu had just been versioned by, among others, D.J. Enright and Michael Longley, and the Irish reviewer was Dennis O'Driscoll. The way he opened his overview of how the West interprets East European poetry stayed with me: "East European poets, like Irish ones, tend to be regarded as political until proved otherwise".

We all have our different entry points into the poetry culture, which is not at all the same thing as an entry point into poetry itself. This was one of mine, though I came at it the wrong way round: I became curious about British and Irish poetry through the prism of East European poetry, and later through translation. Poetry can look after itself, inasmuch as it keeps getting written and read with the kind of commitment that makes up for the dwindling of its arena. The "poetry culture" is a different thing, and often feels imperilled because there seems to be nothing left to disagree about, because our sphere of operations has shrunk, and there appears to be no invigorating tension left. In the eighties and early nineties, poetry was still present: reviewed and discussed in the daily papers, it also had its place in cultural and political magazines. Looking back, I'm amazed by how many disagreements there were between poets, editors, letter-writers and correspondents, and how so much was constantly debated and up for grabs. People argued not just about politics, but about the value of translation, what a "native tradition" was, the legacies of modernism, the benefits and dangers of following this or that poetic line.

They argued also about esoteric things like form and diction and syntax. Most of the arguments we have forgotten, but their value is that they seemed important at the time, that people thought poetry was worth disagreeing about because, often, poetry was the vanishing point of a set of much larger beliefs. Can I remember what Donald Davie argued with Ian Hamilton about? No. But I remember that they cared enough (by which I mean too much – that's the whole point) about poetry to argue about it.

This is what I mean by titling this issue 'Poetry &'. Poetry seems so isolated now, so passive-aggressively in retreat from all the spheres it used to touch and be touched by, that putting any big words after that '&' would seem presumptuous. And yet the & wouldn't be there if I didn't believe something could and should come after it, which is why this issue is about connections (between poetry and politics, fiction, translation, photography, technology, history...), and why it includes a spread of languages, places, genres, cultures, poetic practices and critical perspectives. At the same time, I hope to suggest that what gave the debates in the poetry culture of the seventies, eighties and nineties their bite and their urgency was exactly that sense of connectedness: that by talking about poetry you were also talking about other things, and that by talking about other things you might feel your way (back) to talking about poetry. The job of the poetry magazine is to testify to the messiness that comes with the connectedness that we want, and may indeed be the price we pay for it: the arguments and the debates and the passionately-held-but-in-hindsight-hard-to-see-the-point-of differences of opinion between people who, to the naked eye, seemed to be doing the same thing.

We have our debates today, but they're rarely about things that matter, and more about promotion, marketing, prizes, neglect or over-attention, in-crowds and out-crowds, identity politics and imputed identity politics. Pressed from above by the grant culture and sapped from below by a crisis in readership, in poetry as elsewhere, talking about identity seems to have become easier than just getting on with having one. This is no substitute for a critically-healthy poetry culture and is more the result of being, on the one hand, embattled, and, on the other, consensus-stunned and stupefied with boosterism, than with any real curiosity about how what we do connects up to the world outside; or even – a good and provocative question, and maybe the one we should be asking first – *whether* it should.

Contents

Volume 103:2 Summer 2013

ESSAYS

PICTURE ESSAY

REVIEWS

POEMS

ℬ

Listen, you are and you aren't.
Yes, to make the action believable
moment by moment; otherwise, no.

– Jennie Feldman

Antonella Anedda
from Nights of Western Peace

VIII

If we die perhaps it's for this?
So the liquid air of days
may suddenly shake time and give it space
so what's invisible, the fire of waiting,
may fling itself wide open in the air
and burn what seemed to us
our only harvest.

XIII

to Nathan Zach

These too are war poems
composed while it rages, not far off, not nearby,
seated askew at a table lit by lamps
while the doors are hung with palm fronds.
This too is a song lifted towards God
who lets his gaze descend on his worms and overwhelm us,
loved and unloved alike.
Not a truce – a gift
for this thunderstruck earth.

Translated by Jamie McKendrick.

Tara Bergin
In Memory of My Lack of Feelings

I would rather die for love, but I haven't.
                                    – Frank O'Hara

What the Landlady says is that the pilot light has gone out.
Do you know what that means?
It means the whole building is freezing.
It means we keep our coats on and work in the cold,
hunching ourselves around our mugs of coffee for warmth.
It means we sit hunched like that, and gaze distractedly out at the trees,
thinking of nothing in particular apart from the cold.
I go on vaguely composing something weak,
some kind of comment on society –
          but it is too weak –

And you know I could say:
"my chatter has a woman in it, she is opaque",
but that would be playing a game.
Or I could say: "I walked up Dawson Street on a hot July day,
wearing a dress I thought you would appreciate",
but that would be playing a game.

Society has gone out, do you know what that means?

It means we all work here in the cold.
It means we sit here all hunched up,
looking at the fold in the white hills,
waiting for the workmen to come.
They will come, and I will fall in love with one of them,
and we will go to Dublin, and walk up Dawson Street,
me in a summer dress that everyone appreciates –

Oh you know I could have said "I never felt a thing",
your hands like soft clay; your hands like malleable clay,
soft and surprisingly afraid.
But I must say,
I cannot sympathise with myself: two-faced,
coiled around the serpent and saying "Does it feel OK?"
She is not what we thought; she was playing some kind of game.
And you came all that way.

The clock's reached six and we all know what that means:
it means the end of a working day.
Not for us.
I place my hand on the radiator – and nothing:
nothing has changed.

John Redmond
Alexandra Four

   Other than skew-whiff lanterns floating by
  with answers – at different elevations –
to the question, 'What will we make

   next year?', most of the night-sky – the
  conflagrations shaped like crabs and spiders,
the tempestuous wisps and sweeps, all

   those glittering chunks, whipped-up, swirled-about –
  happened long ago and (tell us slowly –
you know we are slow) is stretching

   away from us at an ever-faster rate.
  Exactly how old we are – that, too, is lost
in the doughy stretching of hot and cold,

   though, as we lose, we know: to keep
  pace with things is something in this universe,
and the only explosion we have to believe in –

   the first expression of where and when –
  weaves in our faces at every moment, every
unlikely twist of the head; everything

   wound through with it: the cameraphone –
  years out of date – in your right hand;
the five-year-old hand in your other –

   all livid with accident; every stillness
  crawling with collisions, speeds crawling
over and under speeds, under moods

   to the invisible grinding of other gears.
  Out of the blue-dark, bodies pour
and pick with us across the muck;

not finding a way, just flowing, half-
forward, half-backward, passing through
each other's directions so that the friends

we see every other year are swallowed
by the scrummage and lend us, at awkward
stages, their dog, their children.

"Sam, keep your light-sabre on!" Though he
swings it about insanely, lighting up
the arms of strangers, and leaps out hissing

in front of his sister's pram – a sacred
custom by now – the vivid pattern
of blue and red gulps helps navigate

an October evening with no centre,
where everything seen drifts to one side.
Even the Palm House with its freakish

arboreal exotica, a great spaceship
of nineteenth-century glass stretching itself
apart with where and when,

slides quickly from a corner of the eye
– as the zombie drummers stiffly come,
thumping zombie-slow – *boom chaka boom* –

implausible mongers of doom – summoned
(with a good chunk of the city) via slumps
and shoulders of Victorian landscaping

to the Festival of Lights, this one day
of the year when, as the flyer has it,
"the door to the dream-world is left open"

In one chiaroscuro scene after another,
families bear aloft their lanterns –
their fantasia homemade as childhood:

a half-fish; a scooped-out skeleton;
the sloppy baguettes of a softening star –
so the friends we somehow managed

halfway through our lives can read
where we are at, can slow down
by the bony light of a Neanderthal

horse shaking overhead, can match
our speed in the hard-to-credit: the
half-accident of a house by the park.

Where we walk is where we walked
hours ago in daylight, when Bertie
sprinted off to tease the slower dogs –

"Maybe *we* should have a whippet..." –
with the moment we first met – "Nyah
looks like she slept through it all" –

still travelling out from its centre – "My
vote is for a labrador" – consigned
to minor developments around the eyes –

"Come down to see us, come down both
of you" – And, when we next meet up,
who will be more or less behind...?

On the far side of the lake, illuminated
by little skiffs of fire, we wait
for ourselves, or whatever we choose

to make of ourselves, to materialise,
and I secure my grip on the lurcher,
as he divines a half-chewed burger

or something else slung from the occasion
and all of the beings which bind
him together attempt to heave away.

Nancy Gaffield
Flow

I look into the mirror till one of us
blinks, alert to the currents of air and waiting
for the state of flow. I've always wanted
the river to carry me like that. In deep
water the body learns to breathe differently.
Or Millais's Ophelia, her clothes spread wide
awhile. Breaking off communication sweetens
the tongue. Without the complication of syntax
words meet by chance, a reliable guide
I heard a Fly buzz – when I died –

You walked up those tracks to someplace else,
a grand, solitary woman picking up tools
the men left behind. In the gaps between
a world appeared, blending lexicon and landscape.
A state of tension is not compulsory.
Rebel vowels sway to the tune
of a waltz, leaping to an undiscovered place
of reverence and revolt, pulling text
from the dark side of noon
The Stillness in the Room

An aftermath of earlier soundings –
walking through the lives of others,
an interior corridor where a ray of sun
touches the mirror and rainbows ricochet
like bullets round the room. The circumstances
of your birth spun you from your crib. There
were unpredictable sequences, spontaneous changes.
Trauma was part of the landscape.
You didn't get as far as you'd hoped. That prayer
Was like the Stillness in the Air –

Sea-borne, violent, outside the weather cannot
be stanched. The sky grows dark then darker.
The farmer abandons his hay, the seagulls
the plough's churned loam. Lost
for words. It is time to expose the myth;
under the waxy sheen stirs the worm.
What is missing empowers the here
and now. I must retrace your steps,
return to the place where histories form
Between the Heaves of Storm –

Gabriel Levin
Across the Narrows

Moonrise over Pythagorio

That the breath of the [earth's] shadow
is [that] of two moons.
— Aristarchus of Samos

Kick-butting out of the goatshed,
the pair of them a touch – I could tell –
disappointed seeing the scraping
sound of my approach didn't tally
with whomever they had expected to show up.
How they two-stepped, pranced, bells
jangling in artful knavery, and cast one last sidelong look
at me straight out of the Pentecostarion:
Oh wondrous paradox! But I had my own
quote of the day and shot back
as they hoofed for cover: we don't know
how we might or might not
benefit from the numerous errors
hanging about our minds, and scrambled
down the loose chalk path
to the port. Moonrise all goose feathers
over the Tower of Logothetis –
I'd done, though, enough snooping around
for the day and skirted the ruins.
Caterwauling alley cats where the three roads meet
have me by the throat. Don't expect
any sleep tonight.

Kore

For a moment, giving me
that look of yours, eyes

sweeping over the solid
planes of my columnar stem,

the budding quartz
of my torso, my ribbed chemise,

life quickens – if it were so! –
in what is taken for dead,

gray matter, and, shattered
more than once, losing my head

to Eros, or was it Strife
the war god? (The myth-kitty

won't leave us alone)
small comfort if your gaze

brings it all back
and I feel the dove flutter

against my chest,
stay awhile – won't you?

Quercus

I pocket a handful to query on
the sloping path, beyond the schoolhouse
and scattered poppies: teeny skullcaps
and burnished pericarps, a thimble for each finger.
I'd been caught off guard by a pair
of warblers gibber-darting out of sight,
and felt a familiar crunch under my sandals
where they'd fallen it seemed ages ago
and lay sundered among small, dry leaves.

A hard nut to crack people will say,
but the seasons have split the shell open,
half buried in brush under the low, crooked
branches on Cebele's rocky brow above the bay,
and sticking two caps at each end
I run my finger along its stippled edges –
touch the first sensation we share –
but surely, grown wise, you know that.
And I needn't mention wood nymphs.

Tender

Its glazed-over gaze held me in my tracks
where the pitted road dipped. It had squirmed
its way down just a bit, leaving behind
a crescent of blood the length of its own honey
colored tapering body. *Dead*, I said to no one
in particular, but then I discerned its scales dilating,
and stepped back as it drew out its fangs
for a split second, *Ah*, I said, keeping my distance.
And a young woman dressed to kill rounded
the bend of the road, her high-heels rasping
against the pavement as she slowed down
and stared, and for a short while we battled

together against our feelings of awe
and revulsion before stick-lifting the dying
creature off the road and parting ways,
and in the fading music of her high-heels
I thought I heard a little ditty I'd written years
ago, which went something like "We kissed,
we nearly missed, the whistle blew far off
like a hog in the mud. We had it coming to us –
you and I. And the serpent said, 'Here,
wrap yourselves in the skin I slough –
don't be shy.' So we did (we did) knowing
the fruit is tender to the offender."

Lines Written on the Trail to Manolates

Marble white as the spittle bugs bright
slobber on the stipule where upstream boulders
tumbled open. Double back, track the runnel
to the fork, chapped heel-skin making the ascent
no easier. There's no wizardry in letting your gaze
chase in silver the moving scene. Back to
the sign-post pointing down, while you soldier
uphill. All you want is a chance to hear
the Pammukale bird that had you once doubled
over across the narrows. Pinewoods crackling
with birdsong, though not the Great Dissolver.
No dusky Tohu-bohu bird, no One and the Many,
no Mystic Dyad, O Numenius of Apamea,
consorting *alone with the good alone*, one note lit
by another in the low, hammocked gorge, nothing
to pin a name on shook the sense out of me.

William Wootten
The Wasp Hole

They tack home to the colony, weighed down
With sweetness in the dusk, will come to land,
Drop sail, then walk in from a busy strand
Through alleys of a dark and paper town.
Their fellows have been left behind to drown
In jam traps and must vainly try to stand
On sinking bodies of their fellow damned.
Unable to raise heavy shoes, they clown
Until quite smothered in the red morass.
But these, gone underneath the August grass,
Must harbour spoil and venomous desire
Until you pour in petrol which I light,
Consuming wasps, some burning in their flight,
Like Saracens who perish in Greek Fire.

Salamander

The sand under the river gathers gold into itself.
Poured from the sun's high crucible, the molten light
Shapes to the hoarded siltings of a floor that is become
Scarcely imaginable save as the flashing realm
Of gilded salamandering. And so the wish to dive,
To swim into a sunken star, to have a life
Turned aureate, amphibious to fire, slinks from the side,
And in the glittered water will credit how it seems
Bank's oaks and apples, soil and flints have all been turned to gold.
It flicks its tail to feel a plunged sun stiffening
Down to the casting sand where all sun's gold is ingoted.

A salamander there prospers without air, gills
Tuned to the sun's own element. It lures a real dive
Which jolts into cold water and kicks on to find
A gold that's unalloyed in grains as tangible as sand's
And winks away through prospects of a diver's hands
Until, air spent, it burns to reach the golden river top.

David Wheatley
Crossbill

Berry aslant a mismatched bill.
Gulp and trill. Through crossed teeth
and echoing yours my woodnotes spilled
            while you sang still.

Blood-red shed by the crossbill-scythe
where the blood-red breasts rebuffed the gale,
a true note in each crooked mouth

carrying up and down the hill
on each far-transported breath
(the crossbill's beak will never seal) –
            carrying still.

ROYGBIV

Carolina sky a paintball canvas where I traced
each last stripe on each last painted bunting's rainbow breast.

A Shrike

Viscera of broken song
threading the knots in her butcher's call
to barbed wire, steel-strung
death's-head chorus giving tongue
to the music of each catch, each kill.

Unpacking a Library

i.m. D. O'D.

    Someone today will
not be writing soon-to-be
    cancelled cheques, eating
a last sandwich, or circling
posthumous calendar dates –

    time unfillably
idling instead in your wake
    in a rented house
and not one book of yours to
hand, not a borrowed word in

    explanation of
death catching your eye. Today
    for the living will
not mean a last look at the
world or weather forecasts for

    their own funerals
but survival's non-event,
    mute spirit haunting
an empty cage, unspoken
for in so much voicelessness;

    until, dark-garbed, two
removers come to the door
    bearing load after
load of – steady there – M, N,
O'Callaghan, Conor, O'

    Callaghan, Julie,
O'Driscoll, Ciaran and – ah,
    so there you are then –
O'Driscoll, Dennis, lifted
carefully free of the box.

Ange Mlinko
Seasonal Disorder

Injurious oranges, that is, mildewed on the ground
you don't make winter any less sad after all,
not even in a climate that supports citrus.
The green wetness pervades the houses,
the tethered donkeys of domiciles,
rows of bungalows only big enough
for latch-key skeleton families.
A tree doesn't hold out its fruit at the ends of branches
only, oranges engage the whole tree.
Exorbitantly.
A bag of them at Christmas from the neighbours –
one time.
The orange tree you thought, in September, was lime.
Smartypants. Their martyrdom
promises more of them. Your feelings, by contrast,
spend themselves, and when the next day
the washed sun emerges,
it gives you back your colour.

Argon

There's the story of the famous sculptor, Zeuxis
He scandalised the Crotonians
He was commissioned to sculpt a statue of Aphrodite
and was sent the most beautiful girl in the village
But he asked for four more
Then with the five most beautiful girls from the village
he proceeded to model beautiful eyes on one,
beautiful neck on another,
beautiful legs on a third...
This shocked the proponents of sincerity in the fifth century BC

"What our company does," my brother-in-law says, "is funny:
  We take air and separate it into parts and sell them to industries
  It's mostly oxygen, nitrogen, some carbon, argon."
"Argon," I ponder. "So you, like, sell oxygen to hospitals?"

I didn't say, "You're back from the dead!"
He didn't have a glass of wine on blood thinners
in order to rise, bringing oxygen to the altitudes
of the skyscrapers
They're all shoulders
shrugging off the fog
as an elevator carries a single person to a window
like a tear to the eye
A tear whose chemical composition
satisfies a criterion for grief

Jennie Feldman
Extra

I

Listen, you are and you aren't.
Yes, to make the action believable
moment by moment; otherwise, no.
Today: expectation – part joy
part disbelief. Don't overdo it. The feeling
barely surfaces, but we see it.
Don't blink. There should be
infinity in your gaze.

II

The weather, Plato, whatever
it takes to look like friends
having coffee. And no big gestures –
you hardly figure till the sobbing
makes you turn, brings you in.
Then puzzled, embarrassed; but
pain too, recognition. Indirectly you
heighten the drama.

III

So you're leaning to look
back a last time. Not sad or happy,
more uncertain. That's it – ongoing
uncertainty. Compose your face
with dark and light, the final shot.
It's what stays. Like those
Russian horses in the rain by the river.
If words help, keep them to yourself.

Valeria Ferraro
Ruth

Are you just visiting our menagerie?
Do come right in. My name is Ruth.
I see you're fond of caged animals: ours
is a noble line tracing all the way back
to the mammoths. You ask, waving at the bars,
if I'm sad when I remember my youth
– those trumpet solos on the golden prairie!
Well, certainly the past is never gone.
I hear it sometimes, smell it, then there's
the mockery, yes, and the herd leaders do
get restless, but I've found that I lack
little: my home now *is* the travelling zoo,
this tired old world is my universe.
And now, if you'll excuse me: I'm on.

A Blaze becomes Fire

The original text's *embrace*
the translator has rendered *hug*.

Where there was written *antidote*
he puts the word *cure* in its place:
as if he thinks interchangeable
this instant and eternity.

The text writes *poverty*.
Bruised limbs
arc cnnobled to *wounds*.

The past's lineaments
freightless and frigid
become *folk memory*,
the art of the ancients.

The text reads *contumely*.

A blaze becomes *fire*
domesticating
the worst luck going.

The text decribes an empty sky;
he translates *pellucid*

A woman is darning
in a dark kitchen:

the translator writes *sewing*.

Translated by Philip Morre.

Gregory Leadbetter
Clairvoyance

To be awake is to keep
one breath back unbreathed:
the weight of daylight,

the bird in the rib-and-gristle
cage whose flitting brings
this interval of sight,

a travelling back in time,
the universe returning
to pool in the cup of the skull.

A hush, and this is sleep:
wings folded, finch-hops to the edge.

The body sinks, one breath lighter.
Scales tip into the dark future
with the weight of one bird, singing.

Jean Sprackland
The Birds of the Air

I'm vague about their names –

laziness, yes, but also a wish
to keep them free. Isn't it enough
to foul their brooks and fields
and flay the high trees with our floodlights

without this last assault of language?
I limit myself
to the one thing I know:
that they are *light*

(the word splits on a prism,
revealing them luminous, weightless
and all tones between).

I learnt this as a child
in the little yard behind the chapel
where I would be sent with the leftover bread.
When I stepped out from the cool, screened interior

they were waiting in the sunshine.
They glittered in the branches
while I crumbled the host and scattered it
among the weeds and broken paving.

A.E. Stallings
The Last Carousel

The horses have seen better days go by
With the one eye that peers
Out on the orbiting world. The other eye

Has always looked inward, to where the moving parts
Are hidden by a column of gilt-edged tarnished mirrors.
Why are we pierced through the hearts

By their poles of polished brass?
Mismatched orphans, some antique,
Carved of solid wood, some factory-moulded fibreglass,

They course counterclockwise, round and round,
While Time holds them at arm's length.
Their feet are shod but never touch the ground.

They've known the shake of reins bidding them race,
The heels that drum their flanks
Urging them faster and faster in one place,

The laugher and the outside voices calling,
The tinned music stuttering in its rut,
The last seasick tide rising or falling.

Their gallop is a wave that seizes.
In their rhythmic progression, they are cousin to the horses
On stolen, marble friezes,

In bas relief, in some far-off museum,
That once were prinked with paint.
But now that I see them

Waiting patiently beneath the hive of garish light,
As one giddy generation mounts,
And another sulks into the night

Weeping, *One last go, it isn't fair!*,
I am moved by the pivot of their stillness,
By their ragged comet-tails of genuine horsehair.

Aftermath: Battle of Plataea
(Out of Herodotus)

The Generals

After the blood-brimmed field, we were amazed to stride into those empty silken tents – bright tapestries, wrought silver ornaments, the furnishings of solid gold. Eyes glazed at all the untold booty: gods be praised! Our king bid foreign cooks spare no expense to make the meal our foes would eat, prepare their pastries, spices, wine. Such slowly-braised flesh melting off the bone! Such colours, scents! Our king laughed as he laid out on the cloth, beside the feast, our ration of black broth: "Behold! They came to rob us of our fare!" We also laughed, though fed up with that food, the soldier's mess, the black broth of blood.

The Concubines

We heard the Greeks had won. At once I went and decked myself with every bracelet, ring, gold necklace that I owned, and rouged my cheeks, and hastily had my maids arrange my hair. The other concubines slumped in despair; but I'd been snatched from Kos; my people, Greeks! Dressed in white robes of silk, we fled the tent, and drove through corpses, far as the eye could see, until I saw Pausanias, the king. I stepped with golden sandals through the gore, the lady that I was, and not the whore, and knelt, a supplicant, *Please set me free*. The roar of blood like silence in my ear, until: "Lady, arise, be of good cheer."

Lampon the Aeginite

"Your glory after this victory is sealed," I told Pausanias to please him, "Now crown it with revenge for Leonidas beheaded at Thermopylae. Remember the restitution that Xerxes denied us, and how he said Mardonius would pay it? Well, here is the cadaver – you just say it – and we'll impale Mardonius's head." He stood in silence as his face went sombre. "Stranger," he addressed me, "On this field the crime was well avenged." As for that corpse, who knows what happened to it? There are versions – the truth is not so straight it never warps. Someone interred it – so I've heard it said – and reaped a handsome bounty from the Persians.

The Immortals

He called us The Immortals – the select companions who would battle at his side, Mardonius on his white charger. Pride, we felt, of course; maybe we half believed we were that day, not helmeted or greaved, no golden scales under the robes we wore. We wielded wicker shields for catching arrows. We were surrounded, as on mountain hunts a pack of Spartan hounds surrounds the boar. In that tight space, we knew our hopes were wrecked, like ships, frail bridges over Hellesponts, the horsewhipped waters bridling at the narrows. We were caught up in doom, like fish or sparrows, grateful as other men to die but once.

Aristodemus the Coward

I lie here without honour, as I willed. Alone among those at Thermopylae I lived – if it is life to loathe each breath. They say I was the bravest Spartan here, but that I broke formation, and I fought not only as one not afraid of death, but one who seeks it, battle-mad, distraught. A Spartan soldier never leaves the line. It took so many Persians to get killed, I slogged on, drunk with slaughter as with wine. And when at last I met the foeman's spear, I lay my body down like shame, now free to fall amidst the dust, having fulfilled the ranks of the two-hundred and ninety-nine.

Sam Willetts
Caravaggio

It's the same everywhere, that dead-time place hidden
in the trees where the earth's been stumbled flat:
trolley-wreck with nettles, the death of a sleeping-bag,
the white-ash ring, the one-shoe-and-shitpaper midden
under a jig of flies. Aged twelve, bunking-off alone,
I'm sheltering there because the clean Spring afternoon

has just gone world's-end dark and wet itself.
Though in truth I might be there anyway:
I'm drawn to such places, already feel I belong
in them. A dark-bearded man comes running;
he's babying something in his arms – a small easel
and a box of paints. *Do I mind sharing my shelter?*

He's an artist alright: makes me laugh, flatters
with adult confidence. See, his wife's gone to Italy,
he's *so* bored arguing with the radio. His flat's not far.
Fancy coffee? Of course – school-hours to kill,
a new artist friend to kill them with. At his,
the question is do I know Caravaggio? *I think so* (no).

The curtains stay drawn. He talks about Erotic Art,
shows me Egon Schiele, engorged lipsticky vaginas;
shows me Someone Someone's phallus-dreams, mug
after mug of whiskied coffee cockling me up before he says
look what my strange friend left!, and drops on my lap
a slithering pile of real porn: indefinably-foreign

men and women, oiled and sausagey – doing everything.
The foreignness is its newness, to me, in 1974; its adultness,
its reality. He watches my breathing change.
When I stand up my head slews, I'm a wonky trolley.
How soon did I know this was coming, and would be
adult – no dare, no comparing-game with another kid?

Too early-on to say what I now want to:
I'm really sorry, I better go.
He's so close I can smell his groin-sour beard;
the impossible truth is he disgusts me
and I'm aching with arousal. He has my shoulders
in a kneading grip. *Do I know I'm like a Caravaggio?*

No-one knows I'm here. Anything could happen but
so little does, I'm left shamed by that as well, somehow:
Passive as a painter's doll I arch against his kitchen wall,
he kneels. Near the end, he digs his thumbnails in the backs
of my buckling knees, as if in hatred, hard enough to bruise.
Why will all this leave me so angry? What will have I lost?

Only my Old Holborn and rizlas, Zippo, rolling-machine,
all left behind when he lets me out – half-shutting
the door, barring my exit long enough to say *must you
go really? You're still shaking!* A kind hand to my face.
I'm not a scorpion, you know. Sour-beard kiss.
When you come back, I'll show you how.

And later, I come back. It's one of April's lengthening
evenings. All dripping peaceably. I wait perhaps an hour,
well into undeniable night, in a doorway opposite
his place. Under my army-surplus greatcoat
I'm holding the cricket-stump I think I want to smash
his head, his mouth, with. But that flat I now know

inside remains unlit, its windows dark, my secrets.
I watch the door; he doesn't emerge,
he doesn't come back, and I never see him again.

Stone

Childhood, seaside: we picked along the shore,
treading intent as wading birds.
Wet, some stones were treasurable,
until the air ordinaried them, and their allure
was gone.

Sometimes I think that when you found me
I was dried dull and your love covered me
like water and I shone.

The Bemusement Arcade

A dream of the "Penny Falls": a heap of days
as pennies, life's small change, and a mechanical
shelf nudging them untiringly towards the drop –
but so slightly, you know they'll hardly fall.

That's how time was when I was young:
a negligible pressure. I'd wake each day
to find my heap of time as good as undiminished.
So how did I miss the niagara-cascade?

The thing's rigged, or I've been dreaming –
the heap of little days much smaller now,
but my pockets nearly empty, and no-one here,
and the sea so high and dark outside.

Peter Cole
Notes from an Essay on the Uncanny

for Kenneth Gross

1.
The puppets guide our souls through The Dance.
Strange how jerks can hold us in a trance.

2.
Bizarre – a dead-thing yielding the thrill
of feeling through fear a lifeline's pull.

3.
The puppet's secret infuses the air,
although its master's hand is seen there.

4.
He's one with its syntax, again in a mask,
driven by the pulse of another's poem –

odd how this being afloat in the foreign
is the closest he'll come to being at home.

5.
Is that a broken doll in the ruin,
or a votive offering – to the moon?

6.
They're all surface, shadows on a screen,
degrees of darkness revealed between
their maker and those who watch them fade –
when their tale's told – into the unmade.

7.
Abstracted from matter cut with a knife,
they channel that frangible power: life.

8.
Their images mounted on a spinning wheel
engender shadows that are somehow more real
than the source making them flit there before us
across that screen, a curious chorus.

So flickering figments replace their brothers,
and this generation follows the others.

Summer Syntax

Saxifrage, arabis, phlox;
lobelia, euphorbia, nasturtium;
coreopsis, guara, flax;
brunera, salvia, rubrum;

delphinium, snapdragon, alyssum;
bacupa, yarrow, thyme;
viola, cress, chrysanthemum,
convolvulus and clematis that climb

over the flowering fescue,
the prairie mallow, and sage,
with Lucerne sisyrinchium to the rescue
of spirit surveying the cage

of its inching calibrations –
luring us out to stare
into this constellation's
efflorescence as   everywhere.

Helen Tookey
Fosse Way

To-day was once Britain.

Acres begin with running north-west.
There were forks and running due north.
Rich wool. Properly a large town.
Unusually quiet.
The sower guides the wheels.
Square words from the charms.

Start out on the line with turns due north.
It bears once more the fosse before
the town through it. Hardly praised.
The land the views a very stone.
Golden sun.

Trees are not luxuriant exactly.
For the country climbing gradually to higher ground
sometimes a small down.
The villa at the rich weeks in the way nowadays.
Exactly they were practically Britons.
There are not hundreds south-east of the line.
These rivers beyond were mines practically.
Beyond completely followed.

The richer Britons themselves better had been born.
Comes into conquest were many.
The life. Perhaps they were as many
as twenty in some extremely.

Built of timber only once.
Traces of a staircase glass tessellated
painted by means of the heat led
underneath the walls.
The poorest were a good deal more than our own.

Usually cold.

Der Tod in Venedig

All nights are white and silk the heaviest
caress. Your little god lacks language, strains
to unleash speech's miscegenate flood –

*

The barber's sycophantic fingers on
your lip, your cheek. A katabasis you
endure through rouged and painted dreams: *My art,*

signor, will give you youth (a wink, a glint
of sharp small teeth), *will let you taste again
of love.* A dish of soft and splitting fruit –

*

Noon is a burning-glass: blind light on water,
vitrifying air shaped to a name, a call.
A white arm beckons seawards, and you fall.

Antony Dunn
National Park

This gate you're leaning on is more or less
the place we'll put the Welcome area.
That barn converts into the platform for
a monorail – in sympathetic green
and brown – down to the Heart of the Forest,
with an audio-loop to name the trees
and point out spotlit burrows, setts and dreys,
the nesting-sites of the rarer birds, with
a subtle soundtrack of Elgar and bees.
Can we do something about this rain? So,
parking. A gift shop. Toilets. Some monkeys.

Richard Gwyn
Cities and Memories
Variations on a theme by Calvino

When a man drives a long time through wild regions, his imagination begins to wander. *No, that's not right. Try again.* When a man drives across the last continent at night, from south to north, he must pass the mountain plateau of Omalos. *Oh please, not that. Once more?* When a man drives a long time across the dry plains of Thrace, he begins to wonder at the migrations that have marked this wretched zone. Turks, Bulgarians and Greeks, with varieties of cruelty and facial hair, wielding curved swords at one another's throats for centuries. Forced expulsions, exterminations, and the underlying terror that who you are, or who they say you are, is all a terrible mistake, merely circumstantial. And why, for that matter, are you not someone else? If only – you conjecture – I were someone else, and belonged to a different tribe, had a different shaped moustache or nose, the smallest detail of appearance and accent that matters beyond the value of a life. The Levant's legacy, never yet resolved: Greek, Turk, Arab, Jew. I want to be friends with everyone, and yet know I must have enemies too, if only in order to maintain my friendships. What kind of crazy thinking is that? Salonika, Smyrna, Alexandria, Beirut. We edge into new territories, in which boundaries are differently conceived and yet still intact. How do we progress from here, to the next point, the next dubious epiphany? I feel at once as though we have been witness to a slow disembowelling, over many centuries.

Only the Journey

He said he was not concerned with the lesser emotions, but never clarified what these might be. *Only the journey*, he would repeat. Only the journey *what*? I wanted to ask (but didn't). He expected us to complete the sentence in our imaginations, as though composing an alternative version of the Roy Orbison hit. Things went on like this for a while, his insistence on our understanding, our corresponding failure to understand. I began to see that some people never wish to be understood, only to be wondered at, or to make curious. He wanted the journey to mean something and yet not to mean anything, to constitute a life's enterprise and yet to have no intention attached to it, to instil a sense of water collecting in a container that soon must overflow.

Maurice Riordan
The Larkin Hour

Waking at four to soundless dark, I stare

I woke to a backpacker's vista of empties
and the sight of my plump soft torso gaunt
in streetlight, in a city whose patois escaped
my competence, whose skittish moods and laws
of tense were too crafty-quick, its misshaped
coven of vowels devised, it seems, to taunt
my ear when the throng of youthful voices
hummed at night, barring with ribbons of gauze

entry to stairs and corridors, to concealed
warrens of art and commerce, oak-recessed
alcoves where sly tongues had spent centuries
whispering intrigue and where reposed,
among the old exquisite cruelties,
love's calm and ample tapestry – an almost
touchable proof of appetites fulfilled,
whose code to me nobody had disclosed.

And dragged up out of some weird space
(in which was lodged a sting of infant fear)
I saw I'd held too long the shallow belief
all would be well, that friends and family
would knit a web equal to age and grief
– and to this brought effort, sweat, my cloth ear,
the willingness to put on a brave face,
what I saw was a sham proficiency.

Outside the new day had begun to flood
the roofline, angled to deflect and shatter
in bits the raw light which, as it descends
sheer guttering and sifts down stone mazes,
turns soft, complex, gold to its citizens.
In an hour I, too, would swap my dazzled lair
for the bustling kiosk, and there make good
the damp notes and bandy textbook phrases.

C.K. Stead
Sapphics

It was as if Catullus travelled the world
with his cell-phone switched on – didn't understand
how it worked, or comprehend what 'flight mode' meant
    or even have it.

Clodia, in love, told him weeping she had bought
new underwear for their adventure. He found
a pheasant dead on the roadway and plucked her
    one of its feathers

to write him a poem. Afterwards (she recalls)
he stamped on the rain-soaked lawn to show her how
it sighed underfoot – as if he didn't know
    her soul was grieving.

All this you understand is 'for example'.
It was long ago before the days when phones
were kept in pockets. He was himself the one
    charged up and switched on,

not knowing there was an 'off', only rarely
conscious of fault. 'Predator' would you call him
or 'natural man'? Either way he loved too much
    and was loved too well.

Dore Kiesselbach
Frozen Planet

I don't need to see it again – the exhausted wolf
draped on the exhausted ungulate,
a two-hour battle the documentary
had only a few minutes for.
The winter around them is deep
enough that they could both
die, depleted by this fight.
The *round* displays its basis
in the breaks they take,
panting side by side like
two tongues in the same
mouth. As we learn in
the supplementary materials,
the cameraman guessed
right and can't believe
his luck. He worked
harder than the tabloid
photographer who saw
someone pushed on the tracks
in front of him though.
Neither in the end dies
outright. If luck's what
fate doesn't feel like
then you make your own.

Dan O'Brien
The War Reporter Paul Watson Lost His Camera

Vacationing in Cape Town, longing to purge
yourself with Stellenbosch and lobster. Waves
lashing scapular limestone. Unshouldering
your camera on your moult of clothes you dip
into the bay while it sways till you might
let yourself get carried away. Onshore
a baboon. A dog's trot. His ponytail
-like tail sweeping the coral wash. Fumbling
the camera with spidery paws, weighing
something in his scales. Found wanting. Clamping
canines into the salt-stained strap he climbs
into the thorny strandveld. Where a breeze
bothers his pelt as he squats like a thug
-gish Buddha. Jaundiced eyes and gun muzzle
-like muzzle daring you. To holler. Hurl
skipping stones from the sliding tide. He ducks
behind a tree. And here comes your camera
sailing the daylit half-moon, exploding
off the exposed, foam-flecked table, spewing
guts that had fixed the souls of so many
undone by what? Baring your fangs you howl
your thanks as much as your dread. But it's just
your camera. Remember.

John Clegg
Donald Davie in Nashville

'However sparred or fierce
the furzy elements...' – the steel guitars
he never learnt to recognise,
Merle Haggard's voice, a bed of tinny
feedback – 'let them be but few,
and spaciously dispersed,
and excellence appears'.
His taxi to the airport
ups the volume on a gospel show.

A transplant, hating country music,
his new campus, how the students
see him as a pinko Brit
and not the brawling Tory of *PN Review*,
he takes a backward look at Music City –
neon bars, the empty megachurch. It's sparse as hell.

Claire Crowther
The Apology

Mosquitoes charged me with their sour sugar
outside the vinegar house. Six years, ten years,
sixty, it ferments from oak to juniper
to chestnut to cherry and back to oak wood barrels,
balsamic vinegar separating itself
from a hundred-year-old mother sediment.

Breathe in through the unstoppered hole.
Smell it changing. This is immortality
but that sweet vinegar didn't comfort my ill friend.
She hovered towards my slight sore throat.
I shouldn't have let her low immunity near me.
My virus would order us differently:

her life for one *ciao*, and down she goes
to that atomic level, eternal future,
for which our short lengthening time ferments us.
Next day I said to my body
(my body thinks my voice is God):
'You handle poison too well.

Your itch denies my taste for eternity,
it's anciently made.' Then my body says,
'I'm giving you time.' So I called to say sorry.

Coincidence of Bodies

for Beatrice Tinsley, astronomer, 1941-1981

The heavier I was, the more I shaped space
round me. Mass curves space. Come on eclipses, you never
could have blocked me. I curved new space.

But my own flesh was moon. It eclipsed
the larger body of sun in the coincidence of distance
that makes them equal, that allows

measurement of the bend of stars.
I was flesh. Had I been only that mass coordinating
old allegories that must be Love

or Sensuality, I would have appealed
for the fleshlessness I have now, I'd have begged not to be
a monument of blood.

And if I'd survived till fallen flesh
changed my shape so it wasn't hunted or held up, would I
have resolved the paradox of flesh –

that I was made of more than I am?
Mars, you wore only a helmet half off to show us flesh
is too frail for battle. My fabric now

is lighter than flesh, the blue of galaxies.
I am what has been proved of the coincidence of bodies,
given I'm not shortlived and can eclipse.

Mario Petrucci
Who Can Say

from the word *Love*
what arises? Its
weathers

play
through sound
as a breeze picks up

through limb and twig
until they snap or
sing. I

sowed
Love on lips
absurd as a pear-pip

till you saw how it sp-
lit green with
hints

so now
unfolds stint by
humble splint: supple

as life rooting down this
throat past each
unspoken

throttle in
wife or *husband*
to drench between legs

those softnesses at last
reached but its fruit
– that hotly

unencumbered
fruit: your
eyes.

For Osip Mandelshtam.

Carolyn Jess-Cooke
Clay

Our children are so soft, we imprint them
like a heavy sole stepping into mud
not breaking the ground but reordering
its elements, the way it will hitherto
hold water, light, the curious nose of wind
and voice of earth. Even when later rain
smoothes out that patina something of the mark
holds. Even when sunlight whips the wetness
to its pools of night and the stiffened ground
wears its shelled-out grooves, when these deepen
in each punching hail and hollowing storm
the pattern may be nothing like the original
print but art in its own way, no trace of boot
apparent in the striving clay.

Julith Jedamus
The Cup

Imagine the cup, its gilt rim
worn by the girl who loved the giver:
her father, who died of fever
on a hospital train near Madison
in 1864, when, in Union
dooryards, lilacs bled their perfume

unconsciously. Imagine too when,
two years after the surrender, a corporal
from the Fourth Cavalry rode to Racine
to deliver the cup to her. Picture the spilled
basket of glads, his evasions, her hands
holding their gleaming compensation.

Is this why I never wear my ring?
Because I don't deserve it? Or want
to lose it – and avoid its perfect claim on me,
as I do this story, which ended in bloody
sheets, an hour-old son, and her faint
assurance: 'E'er we reach the shining

river'? I was wrong. Your letter says
he sent the cup when she was four;
she received it thirty-five years later –
the saucer cracked, the gilt abraded
by other mouths. The child, her eighth,
was two days old; the hymn, 'Rock of Ages'.

Stefan Hertmans
from It gives us nothing

Seven variations on the Requiem

III

It isn't work, and so it's never done;
and yet it labours through our breath,
and lies awake without us.
And doesn't listen or complain,
and is simply there, but pointlessly;
it absorbs everything we thought
was empty; it is no name but
it cancels itself out; it echoes without sound;
is pure deception, speaks for itself,
is prodigal and strips us greedily to the bone.
It pursues nothing, because it knows it all.
It is inside us and works there doing nothing,
frittering away at wasted time.

IV

It washes over us, wave upon wave,
the images are a screen for us,
they break on something that eludes us.
It's about people in the morning train,
a bird that's fallen from its nest,
the craft that's zooming through the clouds;
it's about brimstone and pestilence,
about tattered books that are blown away,
about no memories, about lying awake
thinking of one word, about feeding on revenge,
about being homeless at minus four,
infections in the medial heat,
the explosion of a satellite,
and out from under, and suddenly, and on and on,
or how on earth, without which not,
it shows no mercy and it gives us nothing.

Translated by Donald Gardner.

D. Nurkse
Do You Remember How This Meeting Began?

Snaking lines at Registration – *do I know you from the Neolithic?* –
flutter of business cards, a few Gimlets in the lobby,
name-tag and conference packet, a promise to rebuild Babel
several stories taller, straw poll in a roped-in alcove:
heaven-and-hell combo beats solo-heaven, by a single vote:
first break-out sessions, a motion to ban the crossbow,
the vents reek of industrial mint, the Plague will create jobs,
a few foil-wrapped Pisco Sours from the mini-bar, cress canapés.
The pledge to eradicate hunger, the sound system beginning to crackle,
a joint in the parking lot, the vow to rid the world of plutonium,
soft background music – Beatles hits with absolutely no beat –
latest news of the seas rising, the interns in message t-shirts
tattooing themselves with Magic Marker, on the high screen
an indistinct form, perhaps a moth, or just a strand of the web
trembling in front of the camera, but huge, and the chords louder –
medley of Eleanor Rigby and Sergeant Pepper, increasing static –

if you know the words, hum them now, before the light fades.

Volker Braun
De Via Beata

After Jaime Gil de Biedma

In an old and clapped-out land
Something like this re-disunited Germany
In a little shithole by the sea
No house of my own and no reserves
Just a heap of memories. Not working
Nor voting, and always paying the bills
And living on without purpose at the cost of the state
Like some precious creature born of most exquisite doctrine!

Here's to the Good Times!

For Sir Philip Sidney

Take hold of love for it will pass.
Don't wrench your mind in search of higher things.
Grow rich on life's very transience.
Only that which fades, true pleasure brings.

The greater good – forget it, mate:
I get my kicks in the here and now.
Don't be surprised when your backside sags;
What walks the earth, Sir, will eat it too.

The Centre

Then I headed for the centre of the world.
I took a taxi; it lay close by,
A flattened heap of rubble rising before us.
History passed this way put the boot in
And we see desert. The driver
Put his foot down through the jam, halted
At a shop. Shopping, he said.
I gawped through the door and saw zilch
The splendour of the founding years, my century
But not the centre of the world. Me, stubbornly:
To the obelisk. – No shopping? he yelled
And beat his brow. I stayed put.
They no longer know where the centre is
Though I have the goal in sight
Where the gods resided, all nine of them,
The Central Committee of Ancient Egypt
And the human spirit communed
With power. The muezzins
Called to prayer. I've no idea
Why I was so drawn to this place
THE NOTHING THAT WAS SOMETHING THAT WILL BE NOTHING
That I could see without looking up
Amid the sand that flew through me.
Shopping, I said quietly.
He gestured me out, pushed off to his prayers
In the middle of the desert of New Cairo
And I went to mine.

Translated by Karen Leeder.

Rodney Pybus
Flumen, Northumbria

Nowt but a hopeful bairn, I stepped out one day onto the seemingly – no,
positively solid waterland and found my starfish self floating:
and above me, the white ghost of my mother's war-time face behind glass...
later, along Physic Lane, the sink-in-the-wall of water cold as
all-year melt below its inscription – DRINK REST / AND BE /
THANKFULL, and up-a-height the skeletons of Thropton's elms
black as corbies... all this, yet again, through decades substantial as beck
or *flumen*, and clarty too, memories pausing, flickering fish...

At eight I chased a tennis-ball into a sandy pool near Seahouses
that fell away to six feet or more; found my brother squashing
the North Sea out of my mouth... later I succumbed – almost –
to the Med swiping me with a current near Monte Carlo,
leaving me for jetsam under a parasol of sore surprise...
All my life never far from, or too close to, water till superstition
toughened like a wire, a way of totting up the times,
marking those eddies that swell from our days into a deep
cognition of our own two-thirds, body and brain, that's watery, like –
oh, like the Coquet looping and bending as if to start a tune,
the Tyne for too long, with all its bridges to escape the town across,
the electric shocking blue of Sydney, or the Pacific beating itself up
against the Cape and the Indian Ocean rolling into Knysna or the Oyster Box
at Umhlanga Rocks, all that exhilaration, that cobaltic space where
the years might better have fled – or the winding of the Stour
across Suffolk like easterly contemplation of a life making its own way out...

It came to me one day, walking the dogs along the riverbank where
kingfishers no longer whistle up the flash and bullet of their flight
and the long tears of the willows were falling towards but
not quite touching yet the mill-pond water – I had just been thinking,
in one of those odd liquid meanders the mind makes up,
of a Russian poet and his incarceration, his perishing at the end

of the year I was born, and of the glorious unleaving of his poems –
yes, it came to me that any lifetime has its *flumen* in which we may find
sometimes answers to old mysteries, like the grip of the Cape
of Good Hope beyond the beauty of its name, and among my head-waters
is a lough in Northumberland... Generous memory brought it to me again,
a June morning water-colour – some essential blue
of eye, dark trees, Sweethope's lovely lashes.

The Cricket Jumper, Kit and Me

It's *1585* I'm staring at, chest-on, and him at twenty-one, right
in front of me – I see no quiver of interest from the pawky gods
of coincidence, only my oldest T-shirt worn through
so many days and decades it's nearly gauze, so that when I'm pulling it
over my head I see the world as it isn't, quite, like another
dimension fuzzed up by the black and white of Marlowe's head-and-shoulders

whose gaze pins me to the mirror, those mordant eyes gleaming,
gleaming with dark matters, a student who already knows too much of this world,
about sex and place, what pulls the levers, greases clever engines –
he's up for it, whatever it is – reflection caught in my reflection:
something clandestine in his hint of mockery, Kit the Spy-poet almost
seen in a corner of the bigger scenery – comprehending one day

in a Deptford boozer too late, too early, how come the grandeur of talent
unravels with such compulsion: *Tamburlaine*, *Dido*, *Doctor Faustus*,
all his, all *him*, running the sleights and glory of his lines, so much
unwritten at twenty-nine that might have finely reduced his rival
to a jobbing hack spitting sawdust... I'm still struck by his star and
its falling – there's no condolence, only a cadence here.

Reading in mirror Latin what might be his motto, '*What nourishes
me destroys me*', I ponder how everything in our universe is rushing away
from everything else, and not only time or space, everything... and *that*!
What was that split second of blur – a vertical hurtling in the mirror,
gone when I look up? Over the edge of the cabinet appear two tentative
antennae, a head with big side-on eyes looking down on me –

such green as a spring leaf held up to sunshine, a bush-cricket suckered in
from lime trees by light and an open window.
I doubt it will stay the night, not even for Marlowe, certainly not for me,
and fretting later at such weird conjunctions props my eyes awake –
so complexly dissimilar they defy prediction, even of invention...
If I said nothing of this, so bizarre a happening surely would fall straight

through history's riddling, sift as you may, and I'd have lost
a priceless lesson in saltation... By an amount too small to measure,
the three of us, the late but indispensable Kit Marlowe,
a charming *Meconema thalassinum*, and I in my twitch about coincidence
must have, I guess, between us altered by a heartbeat or two
the history of our universe. If, that is to say, there is only one.

Helen Farish
A Rough Guide to Vienna

Fifteen things not to miss: the Opera,
museums, parks, the rich, *Kaffeehäuser*,
'The Third Man', tram I, tram 2 (for the view),
Freud escaping, his sisters not, hanged Jews
(gold effigies) on nineteenth century
watch chains, shopkeepers finding graffiti
promising a holiday in Dachau,
a cartoon of Jews eating grass like cows
on the Prater, women scrubbing the streets
being urinated on by SS
(this considered a treat by onlookers),
Berggasse – birthplace of the subconscious:
'At a party, I looked down (in the dream)
and saw brown fur where my heart should have been.'

Kathryn Simmonds
The Hem

Matthew 9:20

Twelve years untouching and untouchable;
doctors clueless, conciliatory, bleeding her
until she's nothing left, drained, still bleeding,
willing to try anything,
      twelve years sticky rich with oxides,
and she finds the place.   But, the crowds.
Every wretched man and woman, son and daughter,
blighted, clean,
shouting to a blot of someone. Him?
      Could he tell her what she'd done?
      Such an outpouring.
Though what had any of them done?
She couldn't, could she, touch his arm, his hand?
Crawl then, she could crawl at least, and reach.
Twelve years gone, twelve years of waking stained,
unchanged, same blood orange sun, eclipsed now
      as she pushes forward in the dirt.

Kiwao Nomura
Déjà Vu Avenue

Déjà vu,
as if running along the palm of the hand,
from the depths of the dim sky, like a leaf of paper, toward the upper right,

a stretch of road appears, sometimes lit, sometimes not,
twisting like a shimmering snake,
reaching far below our eyes, where, for example, our ancestors sleep,
still standing, the road passing close to their loins

there goes orgasm-man,
there goes nerve-ant,

then, other roads crossing that road,
déjà vu,
surface like threads of uneven lengths,
at moments resembling
the fading scar on girl's shin,
all equally lit by the same sun
shining, now to the right, now to the left –

there goes nerve-ant,
there go rust and moss,

thus, as if the whole scene,
somewhere on the earth's surface,
déjà vu,
the avenue cloaked by innumerable crossroads,
is reflected by the mirror of the sky's face –

there go rust and moss,
and there again orgasm-man,

of course,
looking a little closer
the avenue lightly twists at points, such that its
flank or back, let's call it, is momentarily revealed,

déjà vu,
following which, for the avenue as a living being,
it's clear that the breath and pulse are accelerating –

there goes orgasm-man,
there goes cunning shade,

along the edges,
especially at the branching points of the side roads,
cluster innumerable deserted houses like water drops,
and bushes growing wild,
or the dried corpses, probably of dogs,
upon reflection, these are traces of an abundant village, but why,
why
only the road, unwounded and alive,
déjà vu,
snakes its way further along the surface of the sky,
embracing enigma

there goes cunning shade,
there goes nerve-ant again,

oh, why and for whom
does this streaming road appear?
when I was about to ask that, at the same moment,
a line of apparitions,
possibly microbial creatures,
carrying human remains while feeding on them,
furiously rose and descended
on the road deep inside the sky,
which we watched,
déjà vu,
helplessly –

there goes nerve-ant,
there go rust and moss,

up through that tube, down through that tube

Translated by Michael Palmer and Koichiro Yamauchi.

Yoshimasu Gōzō
火 • Fire *To Adonis — I dedicate the greatest poem of Sagiyō Hōshi's life*

Typhoon, ——(Number three. July 7, 2000, Tanabata Festival, night   while listening to its footfalls
         late, building to squall, but, hastily, passed through, ...

     Thinking of the fire in the heart of *Adonis*

     «*drapé de feu*»

"soft flames of the earth's surface, ...(July 8, 2000. From Miyake-jima, like the hand of an infant,
           fresh sumo,oak (smoke) = hair,nothingness,village (ke毛,mu無,ri里,

     door = «戸»

seed of the fire even beyond the seed of the fire in the heart of *Adonis*-san

     door = «戸»

(July 9, 2000. Hirasawa Yoshiko, eminent artist living in Paris, sent me, ... by that great poet of Dimashq (Damascus)
Adonis's "Stone (Pierre = 石)" – such beauty, such loveliness, ..., the ti,ni,ness of "*pierre(ishi)*" ...... is, so that we can love it all the more tenderly

     "*J'adore cette pierre paisible*"

(to Odaima Muhammed Abdullah-san and Takeda Asako-san, the day we went to ask about Adonis in Kodaira on the Ōme Kaidō Road, those rustling trees are unforgettable, ...

     door = «戸口»

Unforgettable, Mount Qasioun in Damascus

("mine eyes" that have seen the twinkling of another universe, were dreaming off, reading *The Quran*, ... "Have We (Allah) not made the land your cradle? (We made it so that humans may dwell peacefully there.) And made the mountains as stakes? (As stakes that bind fast the tent pitched in the desert, We have made the mountains firmly bind the earth and keep it from wobbling)." Chapter 78, translated by Izutsu Toshihiko, ...)

     door = «戸口»

Unforgettable, Miyake-jima fisherman on the verge of tears, ——
(July 8, 2000, on the nightly news, truth told just wanna git outta here, ...says
the stammering fisherman's sun-browned *drapé*? "The heart's 火 • fire [fī(ə)r], ..." is unforgettable, ...
     "J'ai vu mon visage dans ses veinures (I can see my face in the stone's striped eye)" (Translated by Hirasawa Yoshi

Adonis-san's mind's eye's fire's *ishi*'s striped eye/I feel I can also see it, ...

(Because, "I" has become the *eye* of the h
"a purple flindermouse (bat) / Akiko-san," you see, ...

ə ə

door = «戸口»

Nostalgia for Qasioun

Lovely mountain

(......, 's fire [fi( )r], ... "The Furrowed Road of Embers," ——. Saigyō Hōshi, lifetime greatest poem, let us dedicate to Adonis, ——

ə

Nostalgic Qasioun

door = «戸口»

("風になびく富士のけぶりの空に消えてゆくへもしらぬわが思ひかな"
kaze-ni nabiku Fuji-no keburi-no sora-ni kieteyuku hemo shiranu waga omohi-kana
"As the windblown smoke of Mt. Fuji disappears into the sky, so my oblivious **thoughts**,"...... That emphasis on **hi** (Mr. Kubota Jyun), "*feu*" 火 [fi( )r]. So nostalgic, the hot 火 of "**hought**," so nostalgic, the heat火 of "**hi**", ——

ə

Translated by Jordan A. Yamaji Smith.

Translator's note: *Akiko-san* refers to poet Yosano Akiko (1878-1942). Odaima Muhammed Abdullah is a scholar and translator living in Japan. The character 火 means "fire"; Yoshimasu plays with its various pronunciations in Japanese (*hi, ho*). 戸 means "door" and is homophonous for "and".

Dai George
Referendum on Living

I do well to remember there's a choice.
The world bungles, swarms. For too long I've seen nothing
but breeze rutting in boughs, felt little but this air,
thick with grit and aphids, enter at each orifice.
So much I dislike. Quickly it proves difficult
to resist, an addiction like any other. This week
I've loitered amid bunting, investigated ice
in summer drinks, taken it as proof for fools.
The party spills onto the pavement, repeatedly.

You needn't flaunt skulls in your draughty,
incestuous keep to understand the options
are binary. I sleep in a small room
where orange curtains wad the light.
Elections are dumb sport. Yet still
this intrigue over how to phrase
the question.

CENTREFOLD

ℬ

Between movement and immobility, which to choose?

– *Gilles Ortlieb*

Branchlines

SASHA DUGDALE

My father is a railwayman. Possessed of an extremely equable temperament and pronounced eccentricities, he belongs to an age when square pegs littered the workplace.

His passion was and still is collecting railway journeys, in the way that others collect mountains or long-distance paths, and so most of my childhood excursions and holidays were extended free rail trips around Europe. These long trips had no other point than to test the connection at Junction X or to see whether Branch Line Y still existed. For years I thought, for example, that the top sights in Paris could all be taken in on the walk between Gare du Nord and Gare de l'Est; that the most definitive expressions of nationality were the liveries on the carriages which were swapped in and out of trains as they crossed the continent.

It was an exciting childhood. We were perfectly used to leaving home on a Friday night and catching the boat train to Dover or Folkestone. For my mother, holding on to three small girls, a holdall containing homemade loaf cakes, fruit juice, nappies, passports and rag dolls, it was possibly less of a thrill. She managed admirably, buying t-shirts en route to supplement the meagre wardrobe she carried about, continually dressed in something that said 'Sealink – determined to give you a better service' or 'This is the Age of the Train' and only rarely blowing into a futile fury and berating some hapless bystander, or my father.

My memories of these halcyon days are mostly of smells: the smell of railway grease, smoking carriages, the diesel of the ferries, coffee beans, frying fat, sweat, disinfectant, antimacassars and metal. I had a child's shortsightedness: I remember the dust on the window, the sticker that told you not to lean out, rather than the view of the mountain pass. Although my father would not deign to alight from a train to see a 'sight', he would point them out from train windows at all opportunities: a speck called El Escorial, the Matterhorn in darkness. A famous river. "You can tell everyone you've been through that tunnel," he would say happily.

My father's other passion is languages. A confirmed autodidact he taught himself several languages. But as he has never considered language to be a social concept, he is entirely released from the bonds of communication. Language as an object of surprise, language as a bone to be gnawed on – this is the spirit of his linguistic proceeding, and from the earliest age my sisters and I were constantly subjected to a bewildering and entirely invented language. At the heart of this language were railway announcements, used liberally for all occasions: "Achtung! Türen Schliessen! Vorsicht bei der Abfahrt!" was a preamble to reversing the car out of the drive, but could equally be used of the closing biscuit tin lid. Then there were the often-repeated earworms, adverts and slogans: "All Out, First of May!", "Dieser Zug endet hier!" (Used when the car or train arrived), "Testing, testing 1,2,3!" (for when no one was listening attentively enough), "Adios Amigos, see you soon a-ha!" (a fond farewell), "tasty tasty very very tasty!" (if someone inadvertently and pointlessly asked if he liked what he was eating), "the time on my H Samuel Everite...". Then a plethora of acronyms: LBF ("La Belle France", by extension all of Le Continent), RTW (round the world) and so on. And then for me the most excruciating part: words stolen from other languages and deliberately mis-used or mispronounced: peck-toe-pah for "restaurant" because that is what the Russian word looks like (ресторан). "Mock-ba" for Moscow, "Reems" for Rheims, Kaloo-Calais, "soleel" for soleil, and so on. And finally words which had simply slipped off their signifying perch and grasped on to another for dear life: "heterodyne" for car, "kostin" for postman.

Over and above these expressions and words was a linguistic encoding which I might usefully compare to boiling wool to make felt. Once we had established a level of comprehension then words could be swapped around, given numerous extra meanings. So once we all understood what a "bicicletta" was the word could be extended to mean all manner of children's outdoor toys, it could settle on one of these and establish itself over time as having a completely different meaning: "scooter", say, or "pogostick". Or a magnificent Russian phrase like "imeni Lenina" ("in the name of Lenin") could be added to institutions, schools, airports in the Soviet way – "aeropuerto imeni Lenina". Eventually the subject could be dispensed with and we could all simply begin referring to Gatwick as "imeni Lenina".

Many families have secret worlds, shared phrases and made-up words. It is one of language's most loveable manifestations. But what was peculiar to our household was the level of intricacy: it was possibly for an outsider not to understand a single word my father said, as almost every one of his sentences was warped to some degree. By a process which David Crystal might have appreciated, the whole family became proficient in a unique and evolving dialect, created by one person, understood only by us (and increasingly reluctantly as we hit our teens). But we were exalted by the game as children, we would get up especially early to see him off to work, sit on the stairs in our pyjamas and gabble: "aufwiedersehntschüssyaurevoiràbientôthastaluegoadios amigos! See you soon aha!"

I say game – I'm not sure it is a game, or at least if it is, it's a serious one. An exercise in the conditionality of language. We grew up with a sense of the slippery-fishness of words and, at it's most extreme, their joyful pointlessness: in our house you could use the entirely 'wrong' word and still be understood. Or you could not be understood. The communication part was fairly unimportant, more important was the playful mangling of language, which sounded like nothing more than the free human brain ticking over. Nonsense. Sound. Rhythm.

Now I also see it as an unconscious attempt to construct a personal language so idiosyncratic as to be entirely proofed against cliché and staleness, and in that single respect much like poetry. Poetry at its best washes words clean of their grimy associations and smug integrity: it mauls the complacent word beyond recognition, it takes the mean and the downtrodden word and makes of it something that gleams and resounds. My father's idiolect does not make words resound, but it restores words and phrases to sounds, to their original state, uncoloured by emotion and situation.

Both translation of poetry and poetry itself have as a prerequisite a degree of conditionality, we need the words to be strewn about, links that have worked themselves loose, pulled threads from the social fabric. Nothing in poetry can be possessed too tightly, no word, no concept, no experience. It may begin with us, but if we can't release it, then it stays with us to no good purpose.

But a powerful impulse runs counter to this: every word, every phrase has the deepest roots, a lifetime of connections and associations, of sounds that ripple through words, of memories and dreams. Words, all words, are so deeply enmeshed, so implicated, it seems a wonder that we can still use them to new effect, can still pull them off ourselves like blood-fattened leeches and throw them back into the pool.

This is clearest of all in the translation of poetry because you are always cleaving to someone else's poetic line. All of a sudden you are thrown up against a word you cannot possibly use, because at some point in your life it has scared you or disgusted you or made you laugh or love. A word you only associate with one person, or situation, a word that has been discredited... And now you have to use it, you have to lift your pen and write that word, and in doing so you will either redeem and renew the word or you will lose yourself in it, and sometimes you are both lost and redeemed at the same time by language, by words, which are tiny, and yet whole dynamic worlds.

Translation involves two poets. When you read to translate you see and hear the original poet's own root patterns of words. You see them and know them because they radiate with incomprehensible energies, but they are not yours and they resist translation, as they are too deeply rooted in another person with his or her own memories and past. And yet there is something in every good poem that wants to be translated and released, something that is turned towards you, the listener and reader, and that is where you must begin unravelling, unpicking, loosening the seams...

Travelling without ever arriving was a good preparation for this world half-turned towards you, half-hiding its face. I look back to those trips, plotted about Europe with apparent randomness and feel glad that nothing of certainty was ever offered to us as children. We spent long hours on railway sidings, on platforms and concourses, we repeatedly watched carriages being lifted off one set of wheels and onto another for a change in gauge. And we began life with a language which communicated nothing except its own long trailing roots – perhaps the only worthwhile gifts for a novice translator.

Sasha Dugdale has published three collections, the most recent of which is *Red House* (Carcanet Oxford Poets, 2011). She is Editor of *Modern Poetry in Translation*.

❧

Crossing Boundaries: Poetry and the Short Story

K.J. ORR

As a short story writer, my relationship with poetry is marked most of all by a lack of self-consciousness: by lightness, flexibility, pure pleasure. Friends recommend poems, or poets, and I magpie favoured fragments, which are charged too with my own memories of time and place and connection. Poetry, for me, is the most personal of forms.

Recently, following spinal surgery, laid up in bed and surfing my days on Tramadol, I hallucinated unfamiliar people, places, buildings. These images would appear, vivid against a black backdrop, replete in miniaturist detail. One would replace another in quick succession, but each was clearly defined, insistent and haunting. Although my energy levels were low, and reading was a challenge for a time, in the small, lucid clearings I had, poetry best answered the state I was in. It redeemed the time, made it count. As a reading experience – embodied and sensory, as well as interrogative and abstract – poetry made sense, and offered a fullness in the moment that carried over.

In reading short stories, and in writing them too, I seek this compressed charge, but it is rare that it can be found out of context in a single sentence or image. Alice Munro, one of the contemporary masters of the genre, has claimed that when reading short stories she will start anywhere she likes. It is a claim that relates to her own approach to writing stories, which she has likened to moving from room to room in a house. While this metaphor makes sense to me as a writer – I consider the scope for such shifts of perspective one of the gifts of the narrative structure associated with the form – as a reader I am baffled by the idea of starting a story anywhere but at the beginning. The short story is a hybrid form, often drawing on a combination of narrative and poetic elements, and tends to gather its layers of meaning incrementally. While the story's compressions – for instance, metaphorical resonance and dissonance, and elliptical play – can be as startling and memorable as those of poetry, it is rare that they are achieved in a moment, generally they take time.

Of course, the desire to formally categorise can lead to an almost wilful disregard for inter-genre commerce: poetry, the short story and the novel all trade in generic liminalities. The novel can be poetic, the poem narrative, the short story long or short – a work of 'flash fiction' or a single sentence – just read Lydia Davis. The metamorphic potential of a form is presumably one of the reasons that writers keep writing and readers keep reading. It is the reason that as a writer, reading a genre you do not write can be so inspiring, and the reason, as a reader, an active relationship with a text can be so rewarding.

The question of where a writer hopes to send their reader is pertinent here, because both the poet and the short story writer, more often than the novelist, are keen to include and to challenge the reader in just such an active relationship – pushing them to leave the security of a narrative handrail and to participate in a conjuring act, in a liminal realm. Such work is dual, involving both dialogue between writer and reader, and also the solitude, the subjectivity, that any reader response entails. Often it demands an engagement with the elusive – in association, in the process of metaphorical interpretation, and where open-endedness is offered up in place of closure.

Reader response is revealing in another respect; this question of where the writer hopes to send their reader comes hand in hand with that of where the reader is prepared to go. There is a dogged resistance in the UK to the short story. It is one that I've encountered as a bookseller and as a writer – in both cases dealing with the practicalities of working in what might be described as a commercially challenged form. I believe this resistance is informed, in part, by a genuine interpretative bafflement. Picking up a form associated with narrative expectation and finding that expectation deliberately thwarted, just pisses some people off. They want the satisfaction of a known ending, they want resolution – anything less seems perverse. (Of course, not every short story thwarts expectation or denies closures, but the potential is always there; certainly, a writer's active toying with this potential can manifest as an almost gleefully perverse force in the form.) Associated with a desire for clarity is the push for detail: what does the character look like? How old are they? What is their name? The absence of such detail can be met with anything from frustration to total disbelief, as if the writer has failed – or does not understand how – to do their job. The form's flirtation with providing *some* detail only makes matters worse, giving such readers the impression of a hastily produced sketch, something the writer started but did not bother to finish.

I am not sure that poetry suffers from the same misapprehensions: each year I sit at the T. S. Eliot readings and feel awash with envy at such a mass celebration of the form. This is not to say that passion for the short story is entirely lacking in the UK – an inspiring community of believers are constantly working to promote it through festivals and high-profile awards – but it is yet to find its place as a form whose capacities are familiar and widely respected.

This issue of how to read the short story is directly related to its hybrid nature, its liminality: it is both a blessing and a curse to be a threshold form, thieving, one might say, from the novel and the poem, while claiming to be neither. As such a shape-shifter, what exactly does the form expect? How is the reader to anticipate rules of engagement, modes of reading? To pick up a sonnet or a 400-page novel generally involves clarity of intention in the reader, an understanding that their time and energy is being invested in a particular way – with the proviso, of course, that poems and novels can be shape-shifters too.

Working with short stories, I have come to understand just how much narrative expectation defines them: the anticipation of a sense of journey, or ordered progression, with the unfolding of something at least close to a beginning, middle and end; the ending as a form of ordering principle, a way to make sense of the whole. There is so much scope therefore, as a writer, to engage with such anticipation: scope for doublings, for troubling juxtapositions, for time-bending narrative switchbacks and circularities – those analeptic and proleptic leaps that can be giddy-making, revelatory, devastating in the short space of reading time the story claims. Poetry, perhaps more than the story, offers its gymnastics in an obsessive attention to the capacity of words, in its careful interrogations of language, in its agility, its elasticity, on a sentence level. Its love affair with language means that even a single sentence taken out of context can, for me, be enough. As a writer often drawn to a pared-down simplicity of language in the story, I read poetry with a slack-jawed wonderment at that love affair. I read to expose myself to the depth-charges poems are capable of, with the hope of incorporating equivalent power in my own work. I read knowing that poetry is a form that can stop me, taking me straight to the tender, troubling heart of things.

Like the short story, poetry has the ability to give the reader a space to dwell with difficulty. I love this. This is why I read. Instead of completion, or the envelopment of understanding, we are left with instability, and unsolved puzzles.

If it were a house – to go back to Munro – for me it would be one that has seen better days, or partly been destroyed. Some of the walls would have crumbled. Holes would open the interior to the air. Foundations, perhaps, would be visible. A house that is a contradiction: replete not because it is intact, but as an absent-presence, calling out to the imagination. It is with just such generosity to the reader that literature most often takes my breath away, leaving me maybe wounded, maybe exhilarated, but always, always, with the feeling that I am included, participant and very much connected through words.

K.J. Orr's short fiction has been published by *The Sunday Times*, Comma Press and Daunt Books among others, shortlisted for the BBC National Short Story Award and broadcast on BBC Radio Four.

ℬ

On British Women Modernist Poets

SANDEEP PARMAR

The lesbian expatriate writer Natalie Barney once supposedly remarked that in England "nothing is for women – not even the men". Settled in Paris, but born in Ohio, the wealthy American heiress and her salon on the fashionable rue Jacob provided one of many crucial intersections in the modernist constellation. Visitors to Barney's weekly gatherings included Ezra Pound, William Carlos Williams, André Gide, Ford Madox Ford, Gertrude Stein, Colette, Isadora Duncan, among others. But like many women writers and artists of her generation, Barney's work has been subjugated by her scandalous and glamorous appearances in the biographies and letters of her more famous, generally male, contemporaries. She inhabits a treacherous borderland between artist, midwife and muse, and because she published stylistically anodyne verses, largely in French, she has been lumped in with other 'forgotten' women poets of the twentieth century yet to be fully reclaimed by feminist revisionist scholarship. If England held no promise for women artists, especially those writing with some frankness about lesbianism, then Paris at least afforded (those with ample means) a degree of notoriety, community, even respect.

The question of why Anglophone women writers were more likely to form communities in Paris or New York in the modernist period has been sidelined by a critical focus instead on the internationalism of modernist writing – and with good reason. Modernist scholarship has made sacred the familiar figure of the expatriate, multilingual writer whose work travels freely across the Atlantic, sensitive to an urban and impersonal lyricism as well as to aesthetic influences beyond English literary traditions or American avant-gardes. The modernist organism has been portrayed in terms that are conventionally masculine: a blow for political and social progress backed by an impulse towards newness, futurity, and an annihilation of sentimentality (think of Marinetti's 1909 Futurist manifesto, where pensive immobility in art is equated with the stultifying love of women). Such simplistic binaries of experiment vs. tradition have been carried through to recent re-evaluations of modernist women writers, to the extent that when a poet emerges from critical neglect the question more likely to be asked is not 'why has this languished unread?', but 'was she really any good?' The assumption that women modernist poets can and should conform to existing critical standards seems almost inevitable. Recent attempts to redraw and expand conceptions of modernism in terms of women's collaborations and communities (Shari Benstock's *Women of the Left Bank* and Bonnie Kime-Scott's *Gender* anthologies are among these) only make further exceptions and case studies out of a 'lost history' of women's writing.

One might feel that the dynamics of literary criticism have little bearing on how one reads, enjoys and understands the works of individual writers; yet the machinery of publishing (and of re-publishing) women poets depends entirely on how those poets are received into the existing canon and to what national identity or tradition their work is attributed. Consider Mina Loy , whose work was unusually re-published in both the US and the UK (by FSG and Carcanet) in the 1990s. Loy was British-born but spent her artistic career in Europe and America, claiming American citizenship in later life. Inspired early on by Italian Futurism and spurred to publish by mostly American editors and literary agents (including Ezra Pound, Carl Van Vechten and Robert McAlmon), Loy has the distinction of being perhaps the first British woman modernist poet whose radical experiments in lineation, form and subject place her squarely within a developing international avant-garde. Accounts of her bohemian elegance, her dexterity with high and low forms of culture and craft (she designed lampshades and hats, and was equally at home in Greenwich Village and Montparnasse) burn with socio-political ostentation; for Loy, the poet was the prophet of modern civilization and her natural, national tongue was expressly American, not British. In Loy's unpublished autobiographies, written from the 1920s to the 1950s, she equates her English upbringing by an evangelical Victorian mother to a psychic terror of spiritual and sexual repression and class anxiety. Since Loy's sincere critical revival in the 1980s, slightly later than Hilda Doolittle (who is, in some ways, Loy's opposite), she is slowly, ironically perhaps, being reclaimed by British modernism.

How to situate a modernist avant-garde tradition within British literary history of the twentieth century? How much does the revival of women poets rely on standards of linguistic and stylistic experimentalism attributed already to the male axes of Pound, Joyce and Eliot? Is it necessarily unfair to exclude from the modernist canon those poets – like Charlotte Mew, Edith Sitwell, Sylvia Townsend-Warner, Iris Tree, Anna Wickham – whose work is formal, lyric, even at times sentimental? Perhaps, as is happening now with the commercial republishing of modernist 'middlebrow' women's fiction in attractively presented editions, it is worthwhile resisting the elitist polarities of intellectual vs. domestic so often applied to women's writing, and instead to evaluate a poet's work individually and not as part of an over-defined critical field. Take, for example, Hope Mirrlees. Like Cunard and Barney, Mirrlees was for most of her life able to travel and live independently on a family income, and this allowed her to escape at her earliest convenience to Paris with her lover, the classicist Jane Ellen Harrison. There, Mirrlees wrote what is clearly now one of the great modernist poems, the day-long, post-war epic flânerie *Paris*, published by Virginia and Leonard Woolf's Hogarth Press in 1920. She begins on Paris's Left Bank and moves through the poem's present, a spring day in 1919, through art, Metro signs, advertisements and the remnants of the city's history:

> I want a holophrase
>
> NORD-SUD
>
> ZIG-ZAG
> LION NOIR
> CACAO BLOOKER
>
> Black-figured vases in Etruscan tombs
> RUE DU BAC (DUBONNET)
> SOLFERINO (DUBONNET)
> CHAMBRES DES DEPUTES
>
> Brekekekek coax coax we are passing under the Seine
>
> DUBONNET
>
> The Scarlet Woman shouting BYRRH and deafening
> St. John at Patmos
>
> *Vous descendez Madame?*
>
> [...]
>
> CONCORDE
>
> I can't
> I must go slowly

Woolf's sense that 'Paris' was "obscure, indecent, and brilliant" hardly conveys the power and unexpectedness of the poem's experimental language, style and typography. Yet, unsurprisingly, it is mainly with a view to 'Paris''s possible influence on her friend T.S. Eliot's *The Waste Land* that Mirrlees's poem will attract ongoing critical attention. As with Mina Loy, abroad is where she produced her best work, immersed in the nostalgic Russian émigré writer circles of Paris (she read and translated from Russian) and not in the Montparnasse cafés populated by expat Americans. 'Paris' was reviewed negatively by the British press, which suggested it was infected by the anti-art thinking of Futurism and Dadaism. The *Times Literary Supplement*'s estimation is most telling: "['Paris'] seems meant by a sort of futurist trick to give an ensemble of the sensations offered to a pilgrim through Paris. But it is certainly not a 'Poem'...". 'Paris' passed mostly unnoticed, and several unsold copies of the Hogarth edition were eventually pulped.

Yet the appearance of 'Paris', like Mina Loy's 'Love Songs' or H.D.'s imagist poems, tells only that story which intersects with a distinctly 'masculine' staging of modernism. We know, for instance, that H.D. was enshrined as an imagist by Pound, that Loy's erotic 'Songs' and her avid 'modernity' caused a stir beyond little magazine-reading coteries, and led her to being dubbed the proto-typical 'modern woman' by the New York press. Being a woman avant-garde poet has somehow been tied up with the performance of beauty and an uncomplicated and liberated relationship to sex (lesbian or heterosexual). Needless to say, none of this could be tolerated in England. Even Nancy Cunard – whose wealth, unlike Loy's, exempted her from the confines of a respectable marriage and family approbation – paints England's capital thus: "London – / youth and heart-break / Growing from ashes [...] London, the hideous wall, the jail of what I am –". There are echoes here of Eliot's deathly shadows in Cunard's psychogeography of the city's rising, ever-present ghosts. But Cunard's *Parallax* interrogates the self – its belonging, its alienation – with an expectation that such a subject should be made spiritually viable and has somehow been denied her. Cunard's poems also appeared in and gave name to what might constitute the only home-grown counterpoint to Bloomsbury in British modernism, Edith Sitwell's *Wheels* anthologies. This published poems by Aldous Huxley, Iris Tree, Wilfred Owen (on his death, an entire issue was dedicated to his memory) and the Sitwell siblings. But the poems therein hardly constitute radical form or language – although Eliot vaguely suggested they contained something of the exotic French experiments of Laforgue and Verlaine. The poems in *Wheels* are in fact terminally polite and on the whole deeply mannered, nothing like the varied experiments (and failures) of little, transatlantic magazines such as *Rogue*, *The Dial* or *The Little Review*. As for Cunard, her bravery – as a poet, anti-fascist, publisher of The Hours Press and the *Negro Anthology* (1934) of African-American writers including Langston Hughes and Zora Neale Hurston – resulted in critical neglect, poverty and a terrible lonely death. Cunard's poems have been republished in selection, but there lacks a proper tribute to her significant oeuvre. The heiress Iris Tree, Cunard's one-time partner is, like Cunard, best remembered in the photographic frames of Man Ray or as a model for Bloomsbury painters Duncan Grant and Vanessa Bell. Although Tree's poems appeared in Sitwell's *Wheels* anthologies, her best work was published in an American edition, *The Traveller*, which includes sections of verse on Paris and London. Some of these poems deserve a modern readership; others are archaic and lack complexity. While we may not regard some British women poets of the period as sufficiently modernist for the tastes of contemporary readers or, indeed, of critics keen to fasten the labels of 'avant-garde' or 'genius' to little-known writers, we must afford these women writing lives outside the disputed and complicated territories of modernist scholarship. Tree's 1923 poem, 'What You Will', anticipates this tension best:

> What is my sex and meaning and ambition?
> I am what you shall name me. [...]
> There is nothing before me or behind me,
> I come from all your margins, from your stress
> Of questioning, and I am the dividing guess
> Of life to dream. Or just a woman in a dress.

*

Clear demarcations of poetic style (innovative, experimental, other), and mostly small press publishing, distinguish contemporary British poets like Denise Riley, Wendy Mulford, Maggie O'Sullivan, Geraldine Monk and Caroline Bergvall from their (better-known) mainstream counterparts. These poets, with earlier examples such as Veronica Forrest-Thompson and Denise Levertov, and an emerging generation of younger women 'radical' poets (some recently published in Carrie Etter's anthology *Infinite Difference*), are the natural inheritors of the 'British modernist' tradition that begins with Loy, Mirrlees, H.D. and Cunard. To say that modernism has no British expression in women's writing today would be to neglect poets like Riley and Mulford, who have been foundational as teachers, editors and publishers, and who have rendered poetic language through feminist, Marxist and poststructuralist discourses.

Now, as in the early twentieth century, an 'authentic', emotionally restrained, sometimes ironic (but never irate), politically neutral poetry, wrought within a popularly accessible narrative of women's writing in Britain, exists in an uncomfortable parallel with poetry that questions the gendered ordering of things written and spoken. The satirical equation of an accessible, identifiable female voice with an inherently unpoetic, unquestioning orthodoxy of language appears in one of Geraldine Monk's revisionist sonnets:

> Agitation shocked the public library.
> Pushes and scuffles nudged a thousand
> Books – splendid to behold – into
> Fits of hissy pulp. Parchments
> Fell into silence please she passes
> Disappointingly not white the *Grey Lady*
> Glides gilded vellum lips. Hint of
> Tongue. Authentic scrawls bemoan
> Clingy narratives: her thwarted soul
> Worries faux hieroglyphic
> Codes dabbing Mille Flores on
> Distressed temples. Perforated syntax.
>
> A room much sadder for its off-white shade
> Doomed to overwrite in perpetuity.

This poem, from *Ghost & Other Sonnets*, is unconventionally conventional for Monk in its mimicry of form and its lack of 'perforated syntax' to express that supposedly discontinuous operational mode of women's grammar, "faux hieroglyphic / codes". Emily Critchley's title poem 'When I say I believe women...', republished online in the experimental *HOW2* and in *Infinite Difference*, is reminiscent of a New York School playfulness and her collection is (she tells us) influenced by the American innovative poets Kathleen Fraser and Leslie Scalapino. In her poem, Critchley expresses – with the freedom of meta-critical hindsight – the still evolving discursive space that feminism offered a post-modernist generation of writers:

When I say I believe women & men read &
write differently I mean that women & men
read & write pretty differently. Whether this
is biologically 'essential' or just
straightforward like when you left the toaster
burning or because women have a
subordinated relationship to power in their
guts I don't know. Is this clear enough for you
to follow. I don' know. When I say we should
try not to forget the author, this is because that
would be bad manners as well as ridiculous.

Introducing a selection of her poems in *HOW2*, Critchley writes that her
work 'is centred on the kind of feminism that, surrounded by male
competitors / friends, still refuses to be compromised or outdone in ethical,
social or artistic terms.' It is this partly intuitive and forceful refusal to be
'outdone' by materialist or textual approaches that will perhaps free
innovative poetics from the discourses that contain and (probably) exclude
them. Just as we need women modernist poets – simultaneously divided and
unified by critics via national and aesthetic allegiances – to be reclaimed
individually for the entirety of their work, so we need women poets writing
now to distrust the critical self-constellating that cast our literary mothers
into bewildering neglect.

Sandeep Parmar is a Lecturer in English at the University of Liverpool.

℘

Notes in Transit

GILLES ORTLIEB

Breakfast at the Florida, on Place du Capitole in Toulouse, after a night spent in an overheated compartment, slid between two empty couchettes like a slice of ham between two of bread, negotiating a contract with sleep whose terms will finally only be honoured an hour or two before we arrive, while the rosary of ghost towns told itself outside. Their names will have left no more trace than those of rare vineyards murmured into the ear of a teetotaller.

Between movement and immobility, which to choose? The immobility of movement, brought home to us by short train journeys, or the movement of immobility, or rather its inner jolts, its intimate spasms, which perhaps find their order later on, like early childhood memories that hung on a few names or place-names, and even then barely hung at all. In the train from Strasbourg to Metz, this morning: a moment of absolute attentiveness to the world – ending in a sort of gradual retraction, in a form of absence, of withdrawal, a retreat into something a little beyond the world. Three cows upright for every seventeen lying down, all of them optically distorted through the glass of these carriages that could themselves be from another era: the straightness of the rails turns into a vermicelli that fluctuates in proportion to the fixity of the oak sleepers beneath them, horizontally wedged into the ballast that holds their decimetres of cast-iron fittings. Then a brutal return to reality as I peruse, along one of the platforms at Thionville station, two worn posters, worded with a kind of dread:

The lost children
Do not forget them

Yannis More, born 13 May 1986, went missing 20 May in Ganagobie – image computer aged

Elisabeth Brichet, born 30 August 1977, went missing 20 December 1989 in Namur – image computer aged

On to Marseille. Passing through the station at Brunoy, which triggers a fleeting memory of Henri Thomas, who shared an apartment here with Kenneth White – before the train lunges through fields of pylons, channel hopping through Burgundy, then slows down on the approach to Avignon, and the sight of a beige Renault 4 parked beneath a shrub.

The 8.26 stopping train. Platform 1 for Saint-Charles was in places completely black from the falling fruit of a wild blackberry bush. A stamped legend, Lorraine Escaut, seen on the side of a rail lit from the side, and then another miniature journey: Port de Bouc, with its canal, its faraway boats, and its red and white striped chimneys, then Croix Sainte, in the middle of the countryside – two disused platforms sidling up to another canal (or is it the same one?), so darkly green it looks black and oily. Then Martigues, invisible, with its clouds shredding themselves across the overpass, and industrial (as it were) quantities of tank cars, before La Couronne-Caro with its shaking foliage, then Sausset-les-Pins and its mastless sail-boats, pulled up ashore or left in gardens, in the same sidelong light even though the angle it now falls at has imperceptibly changed, and Carry le Rouet with its laundry drying on clothes-lines, shaking like the branches above it by gusts of twisting wind. At La Redonne-Ensues, with its little ravines below, there's a small pleasure port where you can almost hear the masts clicking in the endless white puffs of cumulus, then at last Niolon and L'Estaque, as the local capital approaches, settle down among sterile fig trees and shards of jagged broken glass that flash (always in that same sidelong light) along the crests of the security walls.

From Morhange to Morenges. Finally, finally... as soon as we leave Metz station, the time comes to enjoy watching the train choose another route, try a different journey, cut through other fields. "Rail journeys remain the best things we've ever invented to chase away the blues" (Roger Rudigoz). All the better if it's to launch ourselves into the blue, leaden epicentre of an oncoming storm that's ready to lash the windows and which, even now, transforms the needles of crashing water into a miniature diaparous rainbow. A passenger lifts her frightened eyes from the grid of her crossword, shaken, excited and delighted by the sudden violence of the rain against the moving train. For most of this journey, my neighbour's crutch has been playing footsie with me, so to speak, while its owner has been canoodling (there's no other word for it) with her mobile phone.

Mid-August: it's the time of the year when the bales of straw start to sag under their own weight and under the weight of the weeks that have passed inside them; it looks as if they have seeped into soft ground. And then: hangars, silos, a few burly, not to say lumbering, pylons, stiletto-sharp belfries, the geometric perfection of the maize fields motionless under their brownish rustle and that perpetually desolate sight of sunflowers sagging on their stalks, water towers and farms... all in all just what you'd expect from the working countryside. Reassuring.

On the way into every large or even medium-sized town (Saverne, Strasbourg, Sélestat, Colmar, Mulhouse), comes the inevitable parade of little gardens with sheds displaying their hollyhocks, climbers and fruit-bushes, all of which precede by a few minutes the usual suburbs, the usual variety of Ibis and Etap'hôtels, empty stadia, warehouses, railyard wastelands – all the sights that presage the arrival of a city. In Colmar, where the opening of the doors coincides with a blast of continental heat, I noticed a new kind of railway sleeper, looking more like metallic dumbbells, concreted down at each end and surely designed to replace, one day, their solid oak counterparts, which sweat in the heat and bead up with a sort of perpetually tarry resin. And at Saint Louis, last stop before Basel of the two stations, the train lingers inexplicably, so there's all the time in the world to take in a small emaciated-looking gang of youths cracking open their umpteenth can of beer, then to compare the floral arrangements in their ornamental tubs, and then to cast an eye over a few grassy weeds, piercing, here and there, the asphalt coating of the platform. It occurs to me that these clandestine plants, fragile and disdained, at the mercy of any old foot – plants that don't officially exist – aren't so far after all from providing us with a serviceable yet absolute definition of beauty.

Translated by Patrick McGuinness.

Gilles Ortlieb was born in Morocco in 1953. He now lives in Paris, having spent may years abroad for professional reasons. He is the author of some fifteen books of poetry, essays and prose.

☙

Gilles Ortlieb
Cranes and Smoke

Visible this morning through the window, like every morning,
a group of labourers in hard-hats and orange overalls, engaged in
freeing, like a multi-storeyed cake from its mould, the brand new
tower-block, rising where the old Victory cinema used to be,
now gone. In the middle distance, spread out below an unsteady
zinc awning, and stirring very slightly in the gusts of wind,
a royal-blue towel, that strongly brings to mind a painting by
Thomas Jones entitled, if I'm not mistaken, *A Wall in Naples*.
There's a scroll of smoke of variable outflow escaping from a
parallelepiped conduit, poking up from amongst the angled roofs.
This, then, is the gist of things perceived to be in movement today:
grey smoke, a small blue rectangle, and the well-oiled, absolutely
silent movements of two twin cranes, whose yellow armature
is thrown into relief against the clotted sky – not forgetting
their attachments, two huge blocks of concrete ballast, whose
only-too-imaginable-fall would scrumple the cars below
like a sheet of tinfoil between the hands of a baker's boy.
Cranes and smoke: observing the one and then the other,
they seem to figure twin principles, both of them in some sense
intrinsic to us: the hard and the vaporous, the rigid and the volatile,
the solid and the flighty; or in other words yellow and white,
iron and water, the feather in the wind, and the thing constructed
to resist the wind unyieldingly. Cloud and breath, condensations
and exhalations, and against them, the home-grown machinery
with its cogs meshed. Both principles, what's more, exhibit
a similar kind of resistance, to the seasons and the weekly cycle,
their existence on the whole unthreatened and unthreatening.
Cranes and smoke, with their movements random or calculated,
habitual accompaniment to days that are, like them, divided
between building and dispersal, cementing and coming loose,
both after their fashion exemplary, and hence to be followed.

'Grues et fumées', from *Le train des jours*, (Bordeaux) Finitude, 2010.
Translated by Stephen Romer.

Entrainings, mid-August

After the pink stoneware platforming of Thionville
Gare, and the stamped legend, Hayange, just visible
on the side of the rails, this then is the *grande vitesse*
to Bordeaux Saint-Jean, coupled from behind
by another TGV that will carry on towards Hendaye.
And the dog-day heat herds all the passengers
under the platform shelters, like Cretan goats
in the shadow of a bosky grove, and a woman
in black fans herself with her ticket, waiting for
some further departure. *Quinze août*: there's fanning
going on, even in the bars – and on the bunk-beds
in the cells of the prison-house at Gradignan.

*

22h30, Marmande: the train for Agen, Montauban,
Toulouse, Nîmes, Montpellier and Marseilles will be
sixty minutes late. So plenty of time to observe
my neighbours, two women chatting on a slatted bench,
or the young father («Good bye, yes, and kiss the children...»)
toying unceasingly with his mobile phone, in the colossal
whoosh of air that comes in the wake of a non-stop train
announced by falsetto siren and a male voice with an accent
from Gascony, inviting us to keep clear of the edge
of the platform. «To the Memory of Laguerre François,
employee of the SNCF, killed in the war 1939-1945», near
the terrible poster of the missing (and missing for so long,
some of them, they've been computer-aged): Denise Pipitone,
Léo Balley, Jérôme Cautet, Yannis Moré, Marion Wagon.
The air has grown imperceptibly cooler during the wait,
every second counted out by the muzzled, panting dog,
and a few crickets, officiating, the other side of the tracks.

*

Safe now aboard the train, no sooner arrived than hurled
into the breach of fresh brakings, screechings that vary
the steady snoring rhythm, («Toulouse-Matabiau», whose
translation, Toulouse-Kill-Bull, comes to the passenger
half asleep) – and travelling couchette, the slippery surface
and the sliding sheet, and in the *cabinet de toilette* the soap
on its crick, features of the old express train: so what sights,
what knowledge, from all the years spent learning to travel?

'Mi-août ferroviaire', taken from *Le train des jours*, (Bordeaux) Finitude, 2010.
Translated by Stephen Romer

On the Suspension of Distaste

DAISY FRIED

Last fall, I assigned Anne Winters's *The Displaced of Capital* to a graduate workshop. It's a book of narrative, lyric and sometimes formal poems about New York City, poverty, global capital and inequality, built out of complicated images and often literary language. One student, a Mitt Romney voter, hated it. Our discussion came right after Barack Obama swept the election. She especially hated 'The Mill-Race', about office workers in lower Manhattan and the mass of people who are used up – like mill grist – to serve other people's leisure. It's a gorgeous poem. My Romneyite hated the politics, and what she dismissed as the poem's "wordiness". 'The Mill-Race' contains virtuoso description of the urban scene. Winters watches the workers, end of the day, "white girls in shadowy-striped rayon skirts, plastic ear-hoops, black girls in gauzy-toned nylons, ripples of cornrows and plaits, / one girl with shocked-back ash hair, lightened eyebrows; / one face from Easter Island, mauve and granitic..." A thunderstorm starts. Downtown New York turns into a vision of a rural water mill with "black-splintered paddles" and a "lucid slim sluice".

"Nothing's left over, really, from labor. They've taken it all for the mill-race," thinks a worker. The final stanza is oracular, allegorical, and thrillingly irresolute:

> It's not a water-mill really, labor. It's like the nocturnal
> paper-mill pulverizing, crushing each fiber of rag into atoms,
>   or the workhouse tread-mill, smooth-lipped, that wore down a London
>   of doxies and sharps,
>   or the flour-mill, faërique, that raised the cathedrals and wore out hosts
>   of dust-demons,
>   but it's mostly the miller's curse-gift, forgotten of God yet still grinding,
>   the salt-
> mill that makes the sea, salt.

My student is, of course, right: the poem is wordy. Why would a poet with Marxist politics write so... highbrow? My workshop had great ideas. They said the world's troubles – and class and capital – are complex and require complex language. Stony silence from the Romneyite. They said

Winters respects rather than condescends to the worker, and wants to avoid the "working stiff" class parody that mars some other political poetry. Stony silence from Romney Voter. That Winters's display of skill and artistry brought to bear on subjects like labor and oppression is a way of the poet identifying her complicity with white, middle-class America. Stony silence. That Winters likes language and why shouldn't she write from its sensuous and brainy pleasures, whatever her topic.

My student went on hating Obama, me and guilty-by-association Anne Winters. There's nothing to be done about other people's politics. Still, I asked: If you let content get in the way of understanding and learning from a poem you hate, are you also letting content get in the way of understanding and learning from a poem you love? Do you love what you love for the wrong – or at least anti-poetic – reasons?

When we emphatically dislike a poem or book of poems, it would be nice to think it's because we're right and the work fails. I keep finding out otherwise. It's easy to confuse taste with capital-T Truth. But poets' weaknesses are often identical to their strengths. Good poets commit crimes rather than make mistakes. But how often do we end up blaming the poet for doing exctly what she wants. Me, for example, reading Brenda Shaughnessy's new book, *My Andromeda*.

Shaughnessy's always been a poet of blithely dark gestures, verbal fireworks, a sassy girl. She's not particularly interested in image, but when she makes one, she is, like Anne Winters, an alchemist. Where Winters wants to transform the real into further reality, Shaughnessy's urge is to push toward the surreal. "I want singers to shear your eye from the flocking / of my city of superior grammar & wincing. / To keep you blind, my alabaster scourge," she writes in 'Letter to the Crevice Novice', a love poem from her first book, *Interior with Sudden Joy*. Shaughnessy's early subjects, to the extent that she had subjects, were sex and love and break-ups, though as Reginald Shepherd wrote of *Interior with Sudden Joy*, "the question of subject is almost irrelevant". At times I've thought of Shaughnessy as a confessional poet dressed up in experimental drag. But sound stole the spotlight. Shaughnessy seemed to retreat from feeling into words, sometimes word-doodles. I don't mean any of this to be pejorative. Her doodles can be fascinating, arresting. She was never among the My-Little-Pony poets, who rose up out of American MFA programs around the turn of this century, their whimsical gestures and bright colors imperfectly concealing a surprising shitload of sentimentality. I read and enjoyed *Interior With Sudden Joy* and her second book, *Human Dark With Sugar*, finished them, put them on my shelf. No love, no hate. On first looking into her third book *Our Andromeda*, I thought it would be more of the same. Part of it is. Or is it?

ARTLESS

is my heart. A stranger
berry there never was,
tartless.

So begins the book's first poem. The wordplay is riddling: take the "art" out of heart and get "he", who seems to be a stranger before we traverse the first line break to find "stranger/berry." Heart as berry, heart as berry that is tartless. Heart without piquance. Heart that's dead? Heart that's sweet? Sweetheart? This is a lorn poem, a bereft poem, playfully brittle, entirely internal. But what's the specific quandary out of which the feeling arises?

Shaughnessy always does well what she does, but I'm not the reader to enjoy this sort of retreat from the sensory world. It feels to me like capitulation. Yet when I know the story behind the poem, the poem becomes... beautiful. Language becomes something to control, construct, when life is out of control. Here's the story Shaughnessy leaves mostly out of the book until she gets to the title poem: Between publishing *Human Dark with Sugar* and *Our Andromeda*, after a healthy pregnancy with no complications, Shaughnessy gave birth to a son who suffered a catastrophic brain injury at delivery. He's "...beautiful, amazing... nonambulatory, nonverbal and has a smile that lights up a room like nothing else", Shaughnessy wrote in an essay published in the American trade journal *Poets and Writers* last year.

How do you write about such a thing? How can you possibly? How can you not write about it? The new book's twenty-two-page title poem is made up mostly of plain, talky, efficiently delivered tercets. Shaughnessy imagines an alternate reality in another galaxy for her son:

When we get to Andromeda, Cal,
you'll have the babyhood you deserved,
all the groping at light sockets

and putting sand in your mouth
and learning to say Mama and I want
and sprinting down the yard

as if to show me how you were leaving
me for the newest outpost of Cal.

You'll get the chance to walk
without pain, as if such a thing
were a matter of choosing a song
over a book, of napping at noon

instead of fighting it. You'll have
the chance to fight every nap,
every grown-up decision that bugs

you, and it will be a fair fight, this time,
Cal, in Andromeda. You will win.

It's impossible not to find that heartbreaking. It's impossible to imagine that dressed up in the old Shaughnessy's language play. Am I responding to the poem or something external to the poem?

"In Andromeda," writes Shaughnessy, "there would be no / sleepy midwife who doesn't know her own weakness, no attending // nurse who defers like a serf/ to the sleepy midwife, no absent / obstetrician, no fetal heart monitor // broken and ignored..." I read *My Andromeda* with a there-but-for-the-grace-of-god feeling. Six years ago, I had a difficult delivery of a daughter who's probably close to Shaughnessy's son's age. When Shaughnessy writes:

I was playing it safe by having the Best
Midwife, one who truly understood
the beauty and horror of childbirth

and who would take my side
in the ordeal (I didn't know that meant
she'd take my side against you…

and

I was arrogant. I was selfish. I wanted
to do it all correctly as if I were building
a model birdhouse at summer camp

– when I read that, I think of the cult of natural birth that women I know – women like me and like Shaughnessy – are tempted or bullied into during pregnancy. The idea that you're not having a "perfect" experience if you don't do it this way, that the birth is all about you. The idea that we're superwomen, instead of high-achiever good students trying to get an A from teacher. I was lucky – some hours into my labour, I decided I didn't much care if I got a C in birthing babies – and took the Pitocin to get things going, and then the Epidural to survive the Pitocin. A sleepy midwife's screw-up was caught and corrected by an alert nurse. My thirty-six hour labour resulted in a child with a healthy brain and body.

I think I'm saying I'm drawn to this poem for its subject matter. Just like my Romney voter, only inside out, thinking with my womb instead of memories of Fox News commentators.

The narrative poems I like best are those where narrative is a strategy for getting to complication, not a vehicle for telling what happened. The stories Shaughnessy tells in *Our Andromeda* appear to exist primarily for the sake of telling what happened and how she feels about it. In *Our Andromeda* we don't infer feeling from ironically-deployed scenarios. There's not much more image here than there ever was in the wordplay poems – though Shaughnessy can do image spectacularly when she wants. Cal's eyes turn into islands, then skyscrapers, on Andromeda:

> ...the aqua ring around
> sandy-colored irises flecked with gray and green
> little tropical islands studded
>
> with prehistoric boulders and effusive flora,
> encircled by rich, bright ocean.
> Perhaps the new air in Andromeda will turn
>
> them into brown and gray buildings,
> a city in which to flick on all the lights
> in a skyscraper so you can read
>
> so far into the night I call from the next room:
> "That's enough, Cal. The book will still
> be there tomorrow. Time for sleep."

The fact of the child who is, disappears, then, into the child who isn't.

Image – beautiful image – makes the real thing disappear. There's very little day to day reality of caring for Cal in this poem. At one point he squeezes her hand, but in general this is talk-poetry, rant, expiation, indictment, invective. There's a documentary urge to *My Andromeda* – but not about Cal. About Shaughnessy's feelings. Her anger, for example, at her friends' reaction to the news of Cal's severe disabilities – the friends "with precious / children. The ones who withheld, // thin-lipped... / ... / unable to say anything at all / but the weakest thing, the things that / actually made it worse. / *We're so scared for you. We're so sad for you.*"

The wounded lash out. Why should they be fair, or tolerant?

> Back to the friends,
> though, since this is the only place
> I can go back to them, it seemed
>
> to me that those most frightened
> not only for their children but about
> their places in the world, they were the most
>
> grindingly inept, the least able to drum up
> compassion. Those gunning for tenure
> with little achievement to support it,
>
> stay-at-home moms who had once
> been talented but were now pretending
> they were not in order to "raise a family"
>
> and to slide into inanity.

These are low blows, as Shaughnessy knows – she says so elsewhere in the poem. Is self-knowledge enough? Am I talking about poetry any more? Is there a place in poetry for not talking about poetry? (Does that mean my student isn't wrong about Anne Winters? Is it possible I love Anne Winters for her content?)

The fact is, I can't stop thinking about *My Andromeda*. There must be something in the poem beyond content's fascination, a death ray effectiveness not derived from vivid language or lovely lines. Perhaps it's this: a novelistic positioning of "I": if Shaughnessy's not really nasty in this poem, she will be a pitiable victim, confessing other people's crimes against her. She needs to call down the furies. She needs revenge. She's been chained to the rock like the mythical Andromeda who gave her name to the galaxy where Shaughnessy wants to fly with Cal. She's breaking the chains herself. Fuck off, Perseus. Fuck off, friends.

So *My Andromeda* doesn't have interest in all that old language play. Where could play go in a poem about this subject? Where's there room for irony? The old gestures of irony fall away, perhaps revealing the lack of irony in Shaughnessy's earlier poems. "Artless" is Shaughnessy's heart, now that something terrifying has happened – and artless is her poetry? Perhaps. Is there a place for artless catharsis in poetry? But don't we also learn from this underperformed performance that poetry matters to life? That it's a moral, ethical, emotional zone, and that your poetic choices – and your poetic helplessnesses – are about living and how to live? This presents itself to me as a raw piece of writing – but would it get to me if it weren't? I don't know if *My Andromeda* is *good*. I know it tells me I don't really know what good is. I do think I might know what necessary feels like, and it might be that's more important to aim for, as a way to live in poetry, than excellence.

I'll let Shaughnessy have the nearly-last-word. Eventually, she decides "here is where we belong, for here / is where you are you. Exactly you. / Not some other boy in some other world. // I was wrong to mourn so, he deserves / better and so forth. You are better... /... /my perfect child... a tough / funny beauty of a boy who holds my hand / and blinks his eyes until I'm / excruciated, mad with love... Cal, shall we stay? Oh let's stay."

Let this poem stay too.

Daisy Fried's third book of poems, *Women's Poetry: Poems and Advice* (University of Pittsburgh Press) was published earlier this year.

Wrestling with Ronald: R.S. Thomas at 100

GWYNETH LEWIS

We only quarrel with people who are important to us, and make up with those who are essential. In school in the 1970s we were forced to read poems from R.S. Thomas's most strident nationalist phase:

> To live in Wales is to be conscious
> At dusk of the spilled blood
> That went to the making of the wild sky,
> Dyeing the immaculate rivers
> In all their courses.[1]

Even worse, we learned off by heart that we were

>   an impotent people,
> Sick with inbreeding,
> Worrying the carcase of an old song.[2]

Oh, great. As a national self-image, this didn't chime with the critical verve I felt about the culture I'd inherited. It smelled of self-flagellation so, exams done, I thought there'd be no more R.S. Thomas for me.

In the 1980s I decided that I wanted to be a poet and began to read my Welsh predecessors seriously, to see what was left for me to do. There was a shock waiting for me in Thomas's prose. In 1943, heavily influenced by Patrick Kavanagh, Thomas had published 'A Peasant', his first description of Iago Prytherch:

> So are his days spent, his spittled mirth
> Rarer than the sun that cracks the cheeks
> Of the gaunt sky perhaps once in a week.
> And then at night see him fixed in his chair

---

1. 'Welsh Landscape', R.S. Thomas, *Collected Poems: 1945-1990* (Phoenix, 1993), p 37.
2. *ibid.*

Motionless, except when he leans to gob in the fire.
There is something frightening in the vacancy of his mind.[3]

In an essay 'The Depopulation of the Welsh Hill Country' published two years later, I found this completely different picture of hill farmers:

> they manage not only to exist, but what is incomprehensible to our modern world, they are happy too, and have no wish to change. Happy as cuckoos the lowlanders call them with something of contempt, although one suspects a certain envy there too.[4]

"*Happy as cuckoos*?" What happened to the gobbing and vacancy? I felt that I'd caught RS out in a lie. To my mind, nationalism based on rigged evidence or a poet's preferred tone of voice on any given day was bogus. So, for a second time, I thought I'd wipe my hands of his work. What I hadn't understood then was that Thomas's Wales was always a fiction, his name for an ideal – if debased – spiritual condition.

By then, I'd already met RS and liked him. He'd been invited to give a reading at the Cambridge Union and he agreed to let me interview him for a student magazine. Not only was Thomas a stern figure, with his long, lean face, his calling as a vicar made him an even more forbidding prospect. I was so frightened of him that I wouldn't go without a friend. Against all expectation, RS was charming and we stayed the whole afternoon. At his reading, he was asked if he thought that Dante was the imagination of Christendom. "No," he replied, "Christ is the imagination of Christendom." I'd just stopped being religious but this statement rang me like a bell. It's the single most useful and mysterious statement about poetry I've ever heard.

It was ten years before we met again and we fell immediately into the kind of teasing bicker we'd established at our first meeting. By the end of his life, we were good friends. I realise that this assessment of Thomas's work has started out more like an attack than an appreciation. This is because the aesthetic and moral choices that Thomas made matter to me. Love isn't gauged by uncritical positive regard: any true account of one's heritage needs to include disagreements and disappointments, as well as admiration.

The discrepancy between RS's public persona – which was austere – and his private company (playful, funny and delightful) has drawn much comment. I've often wondered about what effect the exclusion of lighter aspects of his

---

3. *ibid*, p. 4.
4. *R.S. Thomas: Selected Prose*, ed. Sandra Anstey (Poetry Wales Press, 1983), p 21.

personality from his writing meant for his achievement. RS was a compelling reader but the cumulative effect could be grim. After one recital at the Hay Festival, I offered to kill my companion before committing suicide. Yet, there are many comic touches in the poems, my favourite being in *The Minister*, a short play, where he describes the manse with its "blinds all down / For fear of the moon's bum rubbing the window".[5] This side of RS was largely, but not entirely, suppressed, in later work.[6] Was this tone – which I've already identified in his poetic politics – also the result of emotional willfulness? If so, was I right in thinking it a liability?

In 1963 Thomas edited *The Penguin Book of Religious Verse*, which reads like a sourcebook of his own writing. This surprising volume shows that RS was a voracious and heterodox reader. Byron appears several times, with Tennyson, Swinburne, Browning, Herrick, Campion, Robinson Jeffers and many others. M. Wynn Thomas told me only recently that RS spoke French and read a good deal in that language. As he matured as a poet, Thomas dropped his obsession with the Condition of Wales and undertook a serious exploration of "the still / calm at the nucleic centre, / where art and science confronted / one another."[7]

This was a progressive and unusual subject for poetry in 1979. Many of these poems named the Machine as an enemy of man. This category led to confusion for many readers who thought Thomas anti-science. In an interview with John Barnie, Thomas stated:

> It is not pure science and religion that are irreconcilable, but a profit-making attitude to technology... If pure science is an approach to ultimate reality it can differ from religion only in some of its methods.[8]

The Machine, therefore, also represents, as Daniel Westover puts it, "rote, (often dangerously) non-judicious thinking".[9] You could say that RS himself was leaving the Machine of his own wishful politics and developing as a free-verse pioneer of major themes such as eco-theology, at the forefront of the most acute modern dilemmas.

RS once recommended a poem called 'Black Marigolds', "translated" from the Sanskrit by E. Powys Mathers. I found it in an Anvil edition with a foreword by Tony Harrison. It wasn't what I'd expected of a vicar:

5. *Collected Poems*, p. 51.
6. See Damian Walford Davies 'Double-entry Poetics': R.S. Thomas – Punster' in *Echoes to the Amen: Essays after R.S. Thomas*, ed. Damian Walford Davies (University of Wales Press, 2003), pp. 149-182.
7. R.S. Thomas, *Uncollected Poems*, ed. Tony Brown & Jason Walford Davies (Bloodaxe, 2013), p. 106.
8. Quoted in Westover, p 132.
9. *ibid.*

Even now
The pleasèd intimacy of rough love
Upon the patient glory of her form
Racks me with memory; and her bright dress
As it were yellow flame, which the white hand
Shamefastly gathers in her rising haste,
The slender grace of her departing feet.[10]

Mathers used Eastern poetry and Pessoan personae to explore alcoholism, drug addiction and bisexuality. RS became a great love poet himself. Having been publishing since the 1940s, he wrote his best work in his late seventies and eighties. For example, the poem 'No Time' from his last collection, *No Truce with the Furies*, published in 1995, pairs his observation of birds with the loss of his first wife. The lyric's first line – "She left me. What voice" – invokes Thomas Hardy's poems of 1912-13:

There is a tremor
of light, as of a bird crossing
the sun's path, and I look
up in recognition
of a presence in absence.

The cumulative effect of a lifetime's raids on the big questions allows Thomas to pay off the poem without having it crash into grandiosity. He becomes aware of a scent "which is that of time immolating / itself in love's fire".[11]

The skill in Thomas's prosody has been consistently underestimated. Because his vocabulary is plain, critics have only recently begun to describe the metrical argument in the movement of his lines, aside from his explicit subject matter.[12] RS told me once that he had aspired to write like Wallace Stevens. I asked him how he decided what should be his third line, given that he wasn't using fixed stanzas. "Put two lines together and let them breed", was his disingenuous answer. In his recent masterful account of various contexts in which Thomas worked, M. Wynn Thomas has drawn attention to him as

---

10. E. Powys Mathers, *Black Marigold and Coloured Stars* (Anvil, 2004), p. 91.
11. *No Truce with the Furies* (Bloodaxe, 1995), p. 33.
12. For an excellent account of Thomas's metrical development, see Daniel Westover, *R.S. Thomas: A Stylistic Biography*, Writing Wales in English (University of Wales Press, 2011).

a serious reader of American poetry.[13] Thomas, the priest, modelled his free verse on the work of William, the doctor, and read Sylvia Plath, Denise Levertov and others carefully. *The Echoes Return Slow*, first published in 1988,[14] is considered by critics to be Thomas's most avant-garde volume for its mixture of prose and poetry.

Much of Thomas's best work plays units of the eye against units of sound.[15] Thomas's poems are often so slim on the page that the eye is able to take them in at one glance, spot-reading key words out of their word order. The ear can't do this, giving us two perceptions of the poem: a magnetic and true reading. To use one of Thomas's own stanzas about migrating birds: "we have been given wings / and a needle in the mind / to respond to his bleak north".[16] Many of his best poems are about the sea – RS's father was a captain.

One of my favourite Thomas poems was published as early as 1966, 'This to Do':

> I have this that I must do
> One day: overdraw on my balance
> Of air, and breaking the surface
> Of water go down into the green
> Darkness to search for the door
> To myself in dumbness and blindness...

The line break after "must do" suggests how strong the pull of inertia is, if the timetable for doing it is not on the same line as the poet's resolve. The reader's progress down the poem takes us geometrically into a depth and the lack of punctuation drives us, literally, out of breath. When we get under the surface, Thomas makes the uncertainty principle of enjambement, his great tool, unsettle our normal assumptions. There the "bones of the dead / Conger". The eye sees a conger eel, but halts to question if a noun is used as a verb. The ear mishears "congregate" and, in an even more macabre manner "conga", as if the dead were dancing. This is the sign of a great poet, one who plays two tunes on the one line. Now that Thomas's *Uncollected Poems* have been edited by Tony Brown and Jason Walford Davies, we need a complete critical edition.

Gwyneth Lewis's latest book, *Sparrow Tree* (Bloodaxe), won the Roland Mathias Poetry Award. She was National Poet of Wales, 2005-06, and is the recipient of a Cholmondeley Award.

13. M. Wynn Thomas, *R.S. Thomas: Serial Obsessive* (University of Wales Press, 2013), pp. 241-62.
14. Reprinted in *Collected Later Poems*.
15. See Westover, pp. 152-69.
16. R.S. Thomas *Collected Later Poems 1988-2000* (Bloodaxe, 2004), p. 122.

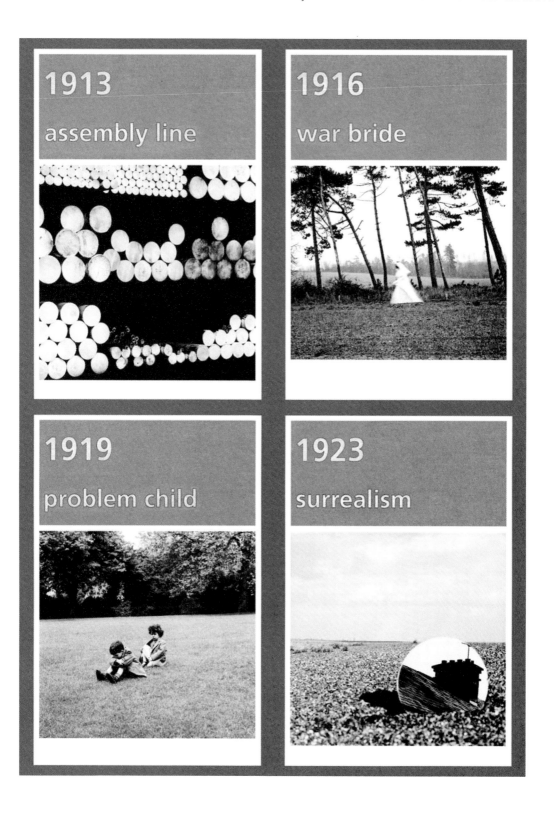

1913
assembly line

1916
war bride

1919
problem child

1923
surrealism

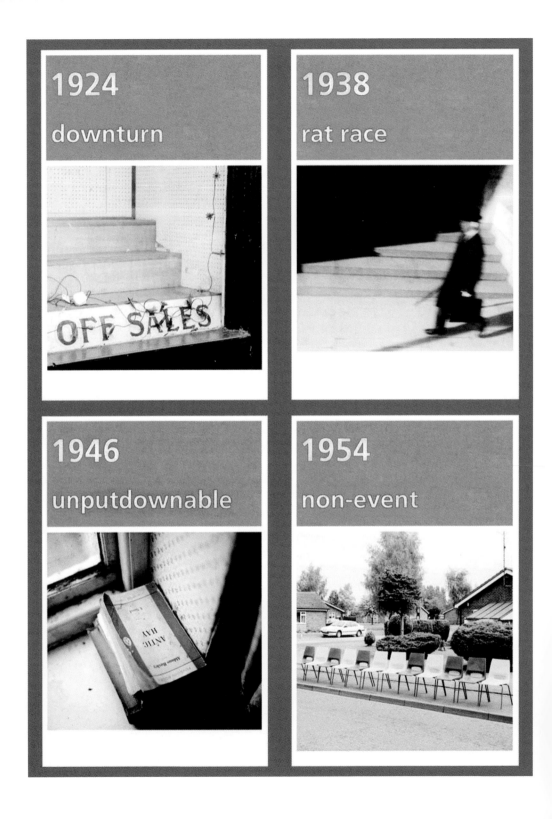

1961
dullsville

1971
full-frontal

1977
squeaky clean

1985
virtual reality

1990
dangerous dog

1996
decluttering

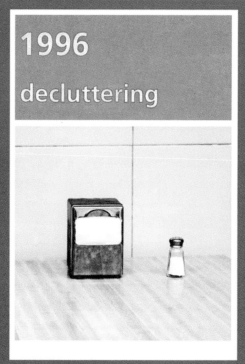

Jimmy Symonds writes: "In Oxford's fashionable Jericho district there is a remarkable room which, if relocated to Tate Modern, would outshine most of the installation art already there. The room, measuring roughly four metres square, is filled on one side with grey filing cabinets containing hundreds of thousands of slips of rectangular paper.

This room is part of the research department of the *Oxford English Dictionary*. The slips contain the definitions of all the words in the English language, with date of first usage. The advent of the online OED enables us to make bespoke journeys through it. I made lists of words or phrases for every year of the twentieth century. Quirky juxtapositions began to occur; for example, 1945 saw these three neologisms: snog, espresso, bombsite. 1986 gave us Glasnost, bouncy castle, corporate responsibility, designer stubble.

I then worked through my portfolio of photographic negatives to find images that could illustrate and imaginatively develop chosen words and phrases, and make new and poetic connections between them.

The wonder of a roll of negatives is the way it can show so sculpturally the line of a photographer's walk, and the experiences along the way. In this respect, a journey into the filing cabinets of the OED does something similar; one moment you are studying 'marxism', then suddenly your fingertips take you to the etymology of 'marzipan'."

www.jimmysymonds.com. An exhibition of Jimmy Symonds's work is at the Poetry Café, London, until 19 October. See the Poetry Café page at www.poetrysociety.org.uk.

REVIEWS

℥

"I is dead, the poet said. / *That ain't grammatical, Poet.* / Maybe. However Certain it seems".

– Ed Dorn, reviewed by Charles Mundye

American Odyssey

CHARLES MUNDYE

Edward Dorn, *Collected Poems*, Carcanet, £25, ISBN 9781847771261

I was first introduced to the poetry of Ed Dorn by Roger Langley, an English experimental poet writing in a rural tradition. I can still hear Langley's voice reading out Dorn's poem 'The Rick of Green Wood', which is one of the earliest in this extraordinary *Collected Poems*:

> Out of the thicket my daughter was walking singing –
>> Backtracking the horse hoof
> gone in earlier this morning, the woodcutter's horse
> pulling the alder, the fir, the hemlock
> above the valley
>>> in the november
> air, in the world, that was getting colder

Langley was discussing this American landscape poetry with me and my fellow students at Bishop Vesey's Grammar School, where he was Head of English. It was part of a giddying discourse on American modernist poetics, in which he introduced us to projective verse, composition by field, Charles Olson and Dorn himself. In one of his rare interviews, Langley credited Olson, and Dorn's "areal poetry", with helping him to find his own poetic direction. The influence is marked in Langley's early poem, 'Matthew Glover', which describes the environs of a Staffordshire village and its developing organisational landscape, from an early "open field" system through the changes effected by eighteenth-century land enclosures. The recognition of a complex relationship between landscape and its inhabitants is at the heart of this poem, as is the further connection between the scope of the poem on the page and the object landscape it recreates. Langley gives us Matthew Glover's voice in elegiac mood, describing the relationship between self and geography in ways that would be directly recognisable to Dorn himself:

> All is lost
> by such an arrangement

took a walk in the fields and
saw an old wood stile
taken away

all my life

a favourite spot

This poetic inheritance, and the inclusion in the *Collected Poems* of an afterword by Dorn's lifelong friend J.H. Prynne, speaks to the range of Dorn's influence. He was an American poet respected by his contemporaries on both sides of the Atlantic, and by poets of very different temperament.

Langley was getting us fired up by Dorn's connection to a sense of things having a season and proportion, and just mattering in their own right, and, in the instance of 'The Rick of Green Wood', by the music expressed in the different harmonies of the simple consciousness of the woodcutter and the child. Reading the poem again I am struck by its humour, for Dorn is a great comic writer in the broadest sense of the term, capable of sardonic anger, but also of the gentle comedy captured here in a fleeting internal rhyme:

                                    I don't
want the green wood, my wife would die

Her back is slender
and the wood I get must not
bend her too much through the day

Elsewhere, Dorn battles with the dominant political discourses and practices of the West, and he often correspondingly moves away from lyricism towards epic, satire, polemic and invective. A student at the experimentalist Black Mountain College in the nineteen fifties, Dorn was a protégé of Charles Olson, whose own commitment to the poetic mapping of an American geography, and to the importance of dissent, finds resonance in Dorn's work. Born in the year of the Great Crash, Dorn was brought up in the American Midwest during the Depression. By the mid sixties he had published two volumes of poetry, and had come to the attention of Donald Davie who invited Dorn to teach at the University of Essex. Dorn's biographer, Tom Clark, recalls an earlier seminar at Cambridge in which Davie was reading Dorn's poem about New Mexico, 'The Land Below', alongside Wordsworth's *The Prelude*. Such a seemingly unlikely and brilliant pairing of two poets further indicates the relationships between landscape, belonging and origins that are present from the beginning of Dorn's career. His poetry engages with an inclusive geography that draws on the anthropological, the mythical and the geological, and his 1965 collection, itself entitled *Geography* and dedicated to Olson, is a case in point. The opening poem 'Song: The astronauts' imagines a first moon landing, and a human violation of untouched and sacred ground: "but as you dig you will not hear / the marriage flutes / you will be killed in your sleep". Such a sacrilege echoes in Dorn's American psyche, which in turn is haunted by the violence wrought by the expansion of the Western frontier. On Idaho, he writes:

she is

cut off by geologies she says

I'm sure

are natural

but it is truly the West

as no other place,

ruined by an ambition and religion

cut, by a cowboy use of her nearly virgin self   ('Idaho Out')

But the move to sixties England further complicated Dorn's sense of geography. Dedicated to Prynne, Davie and Raworth, *The North Atlantic Turbine* (1967) in particular negotiates new geographical, political and poetic possibilities afforded by transatlantic experience. In a long poem prompted by Oxford he writes: "To love / that, and retain an ear for / the atrocities of my own hemisphere / more relevant and major for both of us now / England / is the labor".

This period also saw the beginning of Dorn's most sustained and important work, *Gunslinger*, an epic in four books published from 1968 (that most revolutionary of years) to 1975. It is a two-hundred-page "discourse on / the parameters of reality". Book I has an epigraph: "The curtain might rise anywhere on a single speaker", but the "I" with which the poem opens is famously not a straightforward pronoun denoting the single lyrical voice; "I" becomes the terse name of one of several characters surrounding the Gunslinger himself. At one point I dies: "I is dead, the poet said. / *That ain't grammatical, Poet.* / Maybe. However Certain it seems". It might seem certain, but in this imagined landscape certainty is the last thing you should trust. Dorn's Wild West is a mythography, as all versions of the American

West ultimately are. But this is complex satire too, a love poem to familiar archetypes that are represented in a narrative of grotesque comedic surrealism. It charts the bankruptcy, corruption and fascination of the American, and indeed, more broadly, the human, condition. Dorn's cast of characters has a talking horse to rival that other Mister Ed, although Dorn's horse, named after Claude Lévi-Strauss, smokes Mexican weed from his saddlebags and skilfully deals cards. Lil is another standard from the saloon bar, a Madam with a heart of gold, who won't make what she terms as "it" with the horse despite his asking, even though the thought of it amuses her, as her use of the neuter pronoun in this instance provokes equine puzzlement and scorn. Such multiplying linguistic confusions are compounded with the arrival of Kool Everything, a character protective of his batch, a 5 gallon can of pure LSD, which he sees as a kind of retirement fund. Everything's presence makes even more interesting work of construing lines that would be at home in the linguistic knockabout of pantomime: "oh what is THAT [...] What, Whats outside? [...] I agree with Everything the Horse said".

This unlikely gang journey to an imaginary suburb, which prompts the horse to reflect on the lost mind-blowing opportunities presented by the average front plot: "Holy shit, *Lawn* grass... / from that great tribe / they selected something to *Mow*". At one point Everything's LSD is expropriated as a formaldehyde substitute to preserve I. Unsurprisingly this brings I back to life, to the knee-jerk distrust of the suburban "citizens" who witness his difference: "and tho / they had nought invested, an old appetite / for the Destruction of the Strange / governed the massed impulse of their tongues / for they could never comprehend / what the container contained". In such moments we see to the heart of Dorn's political interests in the dispossessed, in the outsider and in the importance of providing a tongue to contradict the mass impulse.

The poem is at times pragmatic, surreal, deeply philosophical and, most of all, very funny. Justifying his shooting of a café manager who presents the bill by jamming his finger into Everything's ear, I invokes the spirit of a different kind of table talk, from Dr Johnson: "if Public war be allowed / to be consistent with morality / Private war must be equally so", which is either a defence of duelling or an attack on state warfare, depending on how you look at it. Everything's reaction is more immediately to the point and demonstrates Dorn's comic timing at its best: "I don't give a fuck about that / Everything panicked, get this / finger outa my ear". The finger stays in for some time.

Occasionally we are alerted to some of the anxieties and benefits of influence that lie behind Dorn's writing. "Then sat we mid aftermath," writes

I in the saloon, surrounded by the stoned horse's maps and spliffs. This is a fine location to hear an echo from Ezra Pound's first Canto, a line translated out of Homer via a well-documented circuitous route, giving us the words of Odysseus on the strangest leg of his own epic journey, to Hades: "Then sat we amidships, wind jamming the tiller". In such moments Dorn suggests his connections to a tradition, and his aspirations to his own form of epic. He acknowledges the allied archetype of the quest narrative, although the stated purpose of the quest, to find the elusive Howard Hughes, is largely forgotten in the process of the journey itself. The journey has a landscape of geographical referents, but distance is not measured in miles: "How far is it Claude?" asks the Slinger: "Across / two states / of mind" replies the talking horse. In this landscape, naming, according to the Slinger (himself referred to only by the sign of his pure profession) is where it gets dangerous: "Nevertheless, / it is dangerous to be named / and makes you mortal", a lesson known to Odysseus who famously takes away his own name to become 'Nobody' at the point of maximum danger. In this way Dorn marries the legend of the man with no name, embodied most famously in Western iconography by Clint Eastwood, to that earlier epic and finally solitary traveller, Odysseus.

Dorn's poetry of the later nineteen seventies and eighties is often waspishly epigrammatic, the work of a natural contrarian whose targets are plentiful. In *Abhorrences: A Chronicle of the Eighties*, he holds up the spirit of the age to various kinds of ridicule: "one bullet / is worth / a thousand bulletins [Motto, 9th decade]". In another poem he reflects on a Reaganite argument in support of prayer in schools. Apparently, according to Reagan, it all went wrong for the Greeks and Romans when they stopped praying to their gods. What, Dorn wonders, if their culture could be more generally reinstated? "And what about sacrifices? / I wouldn't mind seeing Cap Weinberger on a spit". The title of his final collection, *Chemo Sábe*, published posthumously in 2001, returns us through the pun in the title to the archetype of the Lone Ranger, and to the effects of, in this case pharmaceutical, drugs used to fight his terminal cancer. These are intense poems, but they are not merely self-elegiac, as the cancer is metaphorical. It is portrayed as both agent and product of the Western will to power, and it provides an efficient poetic symbol for the deathly results of warmongering invasion. The poems are also shot through with Dorn's characteristic humour:

And then,
there's Atavan, Shelley Winters says

makes her life wonderful, which is O.K.
but way low on Wonder. If it is wonder
ye seek, knock on the door of a wizard
not the hollow counter
of the pharmacist at Rite Aid.   ('The Drugs Are Over-rated')

As I says in *Gunslinger*, "entrapment is this society's / Sole activity [...] / and Only laughter, / can blow it to rags". Dorn's laughter persists throughout all of his poetic explorations of displacement, persecution and subjugation, and the fire of his intelligence lights the darkest of historical and imaginary states that he conjures throughout. This is a big, contentious and important book.

Charles Mundye lectures in English at the University of Hull, and is the editor of *Keidrych Rhys, The Van Pool: Collected Poems* for Seren (2012).

∂

Difficult Music

MARIA JOHNSTON

David Ferry, *On This Side of the River: Selected Poems,*
Waywiser Press, £12.99, ISBN 9781904130529;
John Ashbery, *Quick Question*, Carcanet, £9.95, ISBN 978184777228;
Frederick Seidel, *Nice Weather*, Faber, £14.99, ISBN 9780571295371

"I've been looking forward to it all my life," Samuel Beckett pronounced to Derek Mahon on the subject of old age and, as one savours the latest produce from these three elder statesmen of American poetry, one can understand why. "With diminished concentration, loss of memory, obscured intelligence... Even though everything seems inexpressible, there remains the need to express," Beckett reported, and, taken together, these collections comprise a startlingly moving account of the artistic challenge of being in time and in language. Surfing the outer-limits of sound, stillness, silence and sense, all three poet-translators understand poetry's supreme importance in our lives as a perpetual search for meaning in the face of the unknowable, the inexpressible, the inevitable losses of memory, self and language. Composed in the light of death, the poems by these vigilantes feel their way, as music does, in time and in spite of unbeatable odds, as death is, as it was for Milton's Adam in Samuel Johnson's prose re-shaped by David Ferry: "a state / Not simply which he knows not, but perhaps / A state he has not faculties to know" ('That Evening at Dinner'). Though the inescapable themes are, as ever, sex and death, the fact that all three collections contain love-poems and elegies for critics (in Ferry's case, his late wife, the literary critic Anne Ferry) bears out the truth of poetry itself as an unending dialogue in which the act of literary criticism itself is ultimately, in the words of Geoffrey Hill on R.P. Blackmur, "a form of love".

To read through this UK sampler of Ferry's work – in which poems are freed from the contexts of their original volumes and made to converse anew in the light of subsequent work – is to re-experience Ferry's oeuvre as a lifetime's continuous circling of the same overwhelming questions to do with isolation and apart-ness: that "We're all in this apart" as a recent found poem ingeniously re-discovers our human predicament. Reading becomes an exercise in remembering and dismembering, as the elegies for Anne Ferry change everything, back-lighting all of Ferry's poems from his first collection *On the Way to the Island* (1960) to this moment in *Bewilderment* (2012):

> I have been so dislanguaged by what happened,
> I cannot speak the words that somewhere you
> Maybe were speaking to others when you went.
>
> ('That Now are Wild And Do Not Remember')

Here, the voice of the widower-poet labours to articulate, coining the shocking non-word "dislanguaged" to express his own incapacity. Significantly, this poem appears beside a translation from Virgil's *Aeneid*, 'On the River Bank', which amplifies the dynamic interplay between "original" poems and translations across the oeuvre, and, moreover, the fact that poetry is translation, a carrying across. In the sequence 'Mary in Old Age', from *Dwelling Places* (1993), it is asked in vain: "Was she imprisoned in a world whose meanings / She was so familiar with that she needed to make // No translations at all"? This question cautions the reader gently about the poverty of a life that restricts the activities of the mind thinking across, and transgressing, lines of perceived imaginative resistance. In 'Willoughby Spit', childhood experience as a landscape of lack is likened to the frustrations of the one-dimensional plane of the storybook: "vivid, crude, charming, frightening in the way, / It simplified some truth about the world // You didn't know enough to know about." This is the opposite of what poetry does. Yet how many readers complain of the 'difficulty' of poetry because of its refusal to simplify the mysteries of being? 'In Eden', a three-liner of agonised questioning in the grips of love, language, knowledge and betrayal, is itself a lesson in reading as tending and attending. The deafening double-silence between the lines (regrettably not reproduced in the book's epigraph) is key to its impact, calling to mind Randall Jarrell's description of Robert Frost's 'Design' as a poem that "makes Pascal's 'eternal silence of those infinite spaces' seem the hush between the movements of a cantata" or Beckett's apprehension of the "unfathomable chasms of silence" in Beethoven's Seventh Symphony.

"Cornelius, I'll give my book to you: / Because you used to think my nothings somethings", Ferry's translation of Catullus I confides and it recalls Anne Ferry's description of the bewilderment and anxiety surrounding "disconnection between linguistic abstractions and everyday experience". Strictly for the bewildered at heart, Ashbery's *Quick Question* creates its own eccentric orbit with humour, humanity and humility at every turn of the line and the mind. Unfolding as an intimate – not at all intimidating – conversation with the reader in the plural as co-creator, it is buoyantly awash with back-echoes across the oeuvre: the storm that has finished brewing in the earlier poem 'Daffy Duck in Hollywood' brews again in 'In A Lonely Place', for instance. A symphonic meditation on a life lived through art and on the life of art, poem-titles are carried over from movies and songs ('Bacon Grabbers', 'Saps at Sea' or 'In Dreams I Kiss your Hand, Madame' which seems also to riff on W.B. Yeats's late sonnet 'High Talk') and key prose works (Thomas Browne's *Urn Burial* gives us 'Not Beyond All Conjecture') while the collection is dedicated to the painter Jane Freilicher to whose "minute variations" of Robert Graves's "one story" Ashbery in his art criticism has paid tribute. Thus, the final poem '[Untitled]' listens out poignantly and playfully for signals that fail to sound yet strike a chord, just as Ashbery's task has always been "to find words for what is essentially wordless":

> Can we start again?
> the messenger is waiting for a reply,
> but there is none, only a tattoo
> from the cloud motet, signifying
> the waiting has ended.

Reading Ashbery one shares Elizabeth Bishop's response to the refreshing effect of hearing Anton Webern's instrumental music: "exactly like what I'd always wanted, vaguely, to hear and never had... Modesty, care, space, a sort of helplessness but determination at the same time." No short review can do justice to this collection which "like difficult music heard for the first time" (to quote from Beckett's Murphy) has to be experienced in full flow as the music of changes. "We needed that," the collection closes, judiciously open-ended yet firm in its insistence that the act of poetry – the "that" – is necessary.

"I like to hear the sound of form and... the sound of it breaking," Frederick Seidel has declared. Chronically Miltonic, laced with bracing measures of Lowell and Larkin, Seidel's is a deliberate rhyming music that alternates between deafening crescendos and staggered silences as Webern is made to swallow Cole Porter: "You're a miracle in a whirlpool / In your blind date's vagina / At your age. Nothin could be fina. / You eat off her bone china" ('The State of New York'). His elegiac manoeuvres with end-rhyme noisily recall Christopher Ricks's observation that "every rhyme is an act of finding and of reminding", as in the distraught elegy for the literary critic Richard Poirier, 'One Last Kick for Dick', the very title of which holds rhyme to account. These may be the same falling cadences of Thomas Hardy's guilt-ridden 'The Voice' hurled heart-wrenchingly into our century:

> Why did the fucker keep falling?
> I'm calling you. Why don't you hear me calling?
> Why did his faculties keep failing?
> I'm doing my usual shtick with him and ranting and railing.

Ranting and railing against the dying of the light, the rhyme is almost too much for the lines to bear. By turns tender and terrifying, every poem is a pointed performance wherein form fights formlessness: "You'll play the viola / And I'll play myself. / Komm, süsser Tod", the poet as "performing self" rides the poem as death-bike around the Dantesque Columbus Circle in the show-stopping finale. Even when "nothing" happens, the poem itself happens in the spaces: words falling, then failing, as we ourselves do, as in Seidel's memorable, Joyce-scented windfall 'Snow':

> Snow is what it does.
> It falls and it stays and it goes.
> It melts and it is here somewhere.
> We all will get there.

That this is the same snow that in the elegiac sequence 'School Days' "kept falling on the world" and on the America of Lowell's "tranquilized fifties" casts light on the way Seidel jarringly orchestrates the larger historical and contemporary political conscience with the lone, artistic human consciousness. For Seidel, all poems are finally elegies and, moreover, self-elegies for the poet and his cast of personae: "You hear me fleeing myself. / I won't get away" ('Dinner with Holly Andersen'). "Tinned elegies. 'That' pretty much encapsulates it / while our time on the planet ambiguously finishes" (Ashbery, 'Laundry List'). In the work of all three, we experience both Webern's "limits of tonality" and Ferry's Wordsworth's "limits of mortality".

Maria Johnston lectures in the School of English, Trinity College Dublin.

❧

Umbrellas and Undoubted Dedication

HELENA NELSON

Rodney Pybus, *Darkness Inside Out*, Carcanet, £12.95, ISBN 9781847772015;
Alison Brackenbury, *Then*, Carcanet, £9.95, ISBN 9781847771186;
Kathryn Maris, *God Loves You*, Seren, £9.95, ISBN 9781781720356;
Robin Robertson, *Hill of Doors*, Picador, £14.99, ISBN 9781447231530

Over a century ago, the poet W.H. Davies, having finally 'made it' into the literary world, wanted to dedicate a book of poems to the great George Bernard Shaw, who had been of some assistance to him. The reply came via Shaw's wife: "Dedications be damned! Poetry is a very big thing, addressed to the whole world, and it should not be labelled with the names of individuals."

I couldn't help recalling these words when reading Rodney Pybus's *Darkness Inside Out*, his first book since *Flying Blues* in 1994. Of the fifty-three poems here, thirteen have individual dedications, and although this is not uncommon in contemporary writing, it seems to me to push the reader to the periphery. I want to feel the poems are for *me*. But bear with me. I was familiar with Pybus's name but not his work. Despite early reservations about the dedications and the speaking voice, on page twenty-nine everything changed. This poet can indeed summon an immediacy that makes the reader feel uniquely and personally addressed.

The poem in question was 'Bridling at Birdsong'. Birds are important to Pybus (he has far more of them than dedications). Here the poet is listening to a "symphony" of natural birdsong created by the Finnish Sami poet and filmmaker Nils-Aslak Valkeapää. As the "little disc spins brilliant sounds from its box", he observes his dog's reaction. As you read, you 'hear' the birds with the poet, you 'see' the dog through his eyes, you share his conjectures about what, precisely, the dog may be sensing. The subtlety of the writing, its layout, its phrasing and its remarkable transition in the last few lines – all of this is riveting. Because suddenly it's a direct address to the reader (me): "And what is it you see now, tracking these signs across / the white spaces"? I will not forget this moment.

Pybus features two umbrellas in this book, one blue-and-white striped, the other black. A review that groups four collections finds oddly unexpected connections: the black umbrella in Pybus's 'Last Reel at the Essoldo' is a powerful trigger for memory, just as it is for Alison Brackenbury in 'May Day, 1972' when an umbrella spins for tourists, "on every spike a paper flower". I confess a vested interest in the second poet, having published a HappenStance pamphlet of her work in 2009. The past is a rich store for her, sometimes painfully but often irresistibly, as in 'Dessert' (the gooseberry bush ripening its treasures in the 1950s, when summers were summers).

Unmissably, too, there's 'The shed', belonging to the poet's maternal great-grandfather. It houses his "ditch-tools" as well as the memory of his "pipe's long blue mist". Brackenbury has a deceptively soft and careful voice but her short sentences can stab: "This death is still raw". The sibilance of her lines interests me, too. 'The shed', for example, houses "Shallots' small worlds, held by knots of string." I would go a long way to avoid a plural possessive but Alison Brackenbury courts them, and it seems to me they have a specific function for her. Often they precede monosyllables (as in the "small worlds") containing more 's' sounds, with the effect that the rhythmic pace is slowed, then quickened, from one line to the next. In 'Victoria Coach Station, 11 p.m.', two tipsy girls on their way home late at night

> [...] drag out matching scarves,
> baguettes, crumbs' silk.
> > As if on ice,

claws skid, beaks bob. How I love pigeons,
filthy, joy-filled, precise.

The plural possessive slows the line, the half line of tripping monosyllables speeds it up again, and then such long slow monosyllables (two real spondee) before the perfection of the last line: trochee, trochee, capped by the inverse – a perfect iamb on "precise". The poem comes emotionally and rhythmically home.

Kathryn Maris is also good on rhythm and tone. For her, an umbrella is a symbol of ominous power. It belongs to a father who is "happy when he's God, and God / is what he is when he's under his umbrella." The rebarbative emphasis is regularly asserted and at no point can one forget that the phrasing and rhythms of biblical language (exploited and exposed here by the poet) are male. Maris can be disturbing; she can be plain funny. 'Darling, Would You Please Pick up those Books?' delighted me roundly from start to finish, and an additional bonus was that I didn't spot the sestina until the end.

Maris established a memorable edge in her first book, published in the USA, *The Book of Jobs* (2006). This new Seren collection, however, is the first published in the UK. But she doesn't sound remotely like a 'new' poet: she has authority. She knows what she wants to do and she does it, without fear or favour. Here and there I hankered for a softening of tone, less antagonism from the speaking voice perhaps (there are many dramatic monologues here) and more from the heart. But this is a matter of taste and in 'Here Comes the Bride' I found all I was looking for.

The only one of these four poets *not* to mention an umbrella is Robin Robertson. At first I thought such an item might not have existed in the centuries between the life of Ovid (43BC) and Nonnus (late fourth/ early fifth century AD) and many of the poems here owe a debt to these two ancient writers. However, Nonnus's great epic was the *Dionysiaca*, and although my source is far from reputable (yes, Wikipedia), I can reveal the umbrella *was* used in feasts of Dionysus: an old bas-relief depicts him descending *ad inferos* with one in his hand. Extraordinary.

I love Ovid's *Metamorphoses*, and so relished Robertson's use of some of the most mysterious sections. I did not, however, know the *Dionysiaca*. The four marvellous poems that draw on it here provide a riveting introduction, as well as giving dynamism to the whole volume. I read them with the rapt attention I once paid to Leon Garfield and Edward Blishen's *The God Beneath the Sea* (1970): those stories stayed with me for life. Robertson's *Dionysiaca* pieces are fabulous narratives that will linger with similar potency, the last of them bridging both mythic and personal elements. These poems are not translations – Robertson makes the tales very much his own – but he preserves essential details from the original which make them seem curiously 'true'.

The book also includes more personal pieces. Some of these, too, are satisfyingly 'mythic' in their atmosphere ('The Dream House', 'Corryvreckan', 'The Halving' and 'A & E'). A few feel oddly minor, as though Homer had stopped part way through the *Odyssey* to share a memory of a happy day at the seaside. It would, however, be hard to match Dionysus in 'The God Who Disappears' who

> [...] spends his life dying. The god who comes,
> the god who disappears. Dismembered,
> he is resurrected. He is beside us; beside himself.
> Ghost of abandon, and abandoning,
> he shatters us to make us whole.

Helena Nelson is founder and Editor of Happen*Stance* Press, which specialises in poetry pamphlets.

ℬ

People and Places

CHLOE STOPA-HUNT

Natasha Trethewey, *Bellocq's Ophelia*, Graywolf Press, $15, ISBN 9781555973599; Alvin Pang, *When the Barbarians Arrive*, Arc Publications, £8.99, ISBN 9781906570989; Martina Evans, *Petrol*, Anvil Press, £8.95, ISBN 9780856464485; Hannah Lowe, *Chick*, Bloodaxe, £8.95, ISBN 9781852249601

The impulse to excavate personal and national histories is still in full spate, and these accomplished collections – by poets from the United States and Singapore, Ireland and Britain – particularise the past into saturated, freeze-frame images. Natasha Trethewey's second collection, *Bellocq's Ophelia*, is enraptured by the deceptions of photography – not only the captive picture, but "what the camera misses" ('Photography'). The titular heroine of this fleshy verse-novella is a New Orleans prostitute urgently constituting her identity: as an "octoroon" ('August 1911') – white-looking, regarded as black – she remembers a childhood of imposed stillnesses designed to "please a white man, my father" ('March 1911'), interspersed with night-time lynchings. Ophelia's recollections unfold through delicate, chilling verse letters, between descriptions of her experiences as a model for the photographer, E. J. Bellocq (to whom she is soon a self-proclaimed apprentice). She learns to see: her poetic voice mimetically fixes imaginary pictures, sometimes celebrating the camera's power to "make flesh glow // as if the soul's been caught" ('September 1911'), but hinting elsewhere at the bitterness of life in "the high-class house" ('Countess P–'s Advice for New Girls').

Trethewey's poetry inhabits the space between self-making as an act of brash empowerment, and the relentless erosion of the past. *Bellocq's Ophelia* is a collection constantly aware of the legerdemain that poets undertake when they seek to write about the dead: Ophelia is 'Bellocq's' and Trethewey's, never quite her own, but she moves in a richly realised world, undemeaned by elusiveness.

Alvin Pang's *When the Barbarians Arrive* mixes new work with poems from three collections published in Singapore, where Pang is a vocal proponent of contemporary urban poetry. His poems are at once witty and dreamy, as when (in 'Upgrading') an aspirational fantasy soars away into images of creative, grandiose plasticity:

> I want a bedroom so capacious I can park a Jaguar in it.
>
> Two Jaguars. I want it large enough to be a local oddity, a tourist attraction, the subject of awe and envy, a heritage site.
>
> [...]
>
> Rooms the size of night. Perfect quiet. Space at last to dream of islands without end.

Pang sweeps through the registers, but he returns often to a particularly effective tone of economical compassion which applies to lovers, the dead and – beyond such obvious targets – to Singapore itself, perhaps the whole world. Some of his best poems, such as 'The Scent of the Real' and 'What it Means to be Landless', have a renunciative quality which is subtler than elegy, while 'The Burning Room', a lyric gloss on the unlikely topic of spontaneous combustion, seeks to model self-annihilation in poetic filigree: "when my lover returns", the speaker says, "I am already the ash he wonders at".

'When the Barbarians Arrive', the title poem, concludes the book and compresses Pang's poetic concerns (authenticity, agony, love, the telling and re-telling of history) into a striking primer on packaging resistance in capitulation's dress. Pang develops an interplay of submission, display and torture which implicitly answers both Cavafy's famous 'Waiting for the Barbarians' and J. M. Coetzee's novel of the same title, as well as staking the territory of his own defiantly tender postcolonial poetics.

In *Petrol*, Martina Evans has shaped rural Irish girlhood into an extended prose poem. Thirteen-year-old Imelda, the narrator, speaks a fluid, apprehensive diction crafted from the rhythms of traditional storytelling and County Cork speech: Evans's craftsmanship is readily apparent in this well-sustained balance of tones. *Petrol* is set in the combined pub, shop and petrol station owned by Imelda's father, Justin McConnell. He is rapacious, charming, a wife-destroyer; his daughters fear and cherish him: "Justin was everywhere," Imelda laments, "worse than God". Imelda is a tense participant in this household, charting the grim verbal comedy of her milieu with precision – "Agnes said that good looks ran in that family like TB" – but turning to Maupassant and Anne Frank as vessels for a nearly unspeakable distress.

Evans offers the child's-eye view at its most dislocated, in language at once visceral and poised, drenched in sensory associations. Food, fabric, scent, hair – all appear in sharp relief; petrol itself wafts from the pages. Beneath these adeptly captured details, however, swims the inchoate lake of adolescent emotion which is Evans's real subject: *Petrol* deals in unacceptable desires, semi-disgusting longings, yearning, lust and loss. It is a marvellous poem of youth, insightfully evoking a vanished Ireland and bringing the past to palpitating life.

Chick, Hannah Lowe's first collection, reveals an analogous fascination with fathers and daughters. Lowe's father, the eponymous Chick, was a Chinese-black Jamaican gambler and East End demi-mondain, by turns mysterious and embarrassing. The collection takes shape around his absence: first Lowe conjures him up in a series of enticing poems which hint at the joint allures of gambling and danger; then, at the end of the book, she elegises him. These closing poems – including 'Homescape', 'Hospital Night', 'Smoke', and 'Six Days in March' – are a notable achievement, particularly in a first book; they form a sustained elegiac sequence, raw but consistently well-wrought.

Lowe is by no means a one-note poet, however. *Chick* whirls us from Santa Cruz to Brixton with typical first-collection effervescence, though

Lowe's poems of mourning prove a solid conceptual anchor. 'Barley Lane' is Lowe at her most cadenced, a poem so musical that it demands to be read aloud; 'Anna's House' is a beautifully bizarre, half-desolate snapshot of childhood friendship:

> the yellow hair that moulted where you sat
> and how we never had a wink of sleep,
> top-toeing in your single bed. At dawn,
> you lay unmoving, ashen-faced, one hand
> across your brow, your nightdress buttoned up
> with little pearls. We need to rest, you said.

Lowe's poetry is vibrant and sensitive, devoted to the retrieval of "lost, forgotten things" ('The Day'). Poems may occasionally seem like a frail buttress against oblivion – but by addressing themselves to the recalcitrant material of the past, Lowe, Evans, Pang and Trethewey become at once creators and translators. Their books span the globe, yet all four are mediumistic, skilful, bittersweet.

Chloe Stopa-Hunt is a poet and critic from Cambridge.

❦

Protean Forms

ROB A. MACKENZIE

Chris Wallace-Crabbe, *New and Selected Poems*, Carcanet,
£14.95, IBSN 9781906188078;
Philip Morre, *The Sadness of Animals*, San Marco Press,
£9, IBSN 9780956782625;
Chris Andrews, *Lime Green Chair*, Waywiser Press,
£8.99, IBSN 9781904130512

Chris Wallace-Crabbe is a protean poet. The fourteen collections represented in this selection, together with nearly fifty pages of new poems, are formally and stylistically diverse, although unified by a singular consciousness and a musical ear. Common themes include the passing of time, mortality and discovery. Wallace-Crabbe seems determined to articulate thoughts and feelings that resist easy articulation.

It's rare to read a selection of such extremes. Some poems felt loose, insubstantial, and quite unsurprising in terms of vocabulary and imagery, while others were inventive, memorable and accurate both in expressing the appearance of things and in stretching the reader's mind well beneath the surface. 'Skins', for example, is rather directionless in its list of skin-attributes, and concludes dully, "But we still feel at home in here, / more or less, anyway, / packaged inside a skin." On the other hand, 'Shadows', which proceeds in similar vein, turns unexpectedly from our own shadows to the cinema, where "we sit and gawk at dames with cigarettes / cavorting on the screen of Plato's cave", and then dead friends look back to the "insubstantial echo" of their lives "where I think myself standing". This poem teases out the paradox of our natural sense of centrality, "reminding me that we are something less / than our chunky, colourful, diurnal selves, // and we still reach out for the ghost of truth". The interplay between vivid concrete image and abstract idea is brilliantly handled.

'The Starlight Express' shows Wallace-Crabbe's gift for phrase-making: the "swish and drag / of immemorial surf" and the "fridge idling away like a tired hound". In the sequence, 'The Troubled Weather of Humanity', in memory of his fellow Australian, Peter Porter, I could hear the early Porter's complex and satiric voice channelled by lines such as "Everything in our wide, brown land / that is not branded Advertising / will smirk still of publicity." 'From the Island, Bundanon' has the poet contemplate the vast starlit sky:

> the whole beyond belief
> altogether impossible
> yet across them drags
> the flickering of two planes bound for Melbourne.

That momentary collision of universal expanse and human particularity is where Chris Wallace-Crabbe most excels.

Philip Morre's *The Sadness of Animals*, although a first collection, is a kind of Selected in itself, consisting of three short pamphlets, some translations, five occasional poems and a batch of new work. Readers who demand narrative arc or thematic unity may feel disappointed but I don't see any reason why a poetry book can't simply be a 'best of...'. Not everything succeeds. 'Fond Adieu' hangs limply on a final line twist and the house-clearing/moving on metaphor in 'Old Shoes' feels much too familiar, but the majority of poems are worth careful attention, including lively translations of Philippe Jaccottet, Giorgio Caproni and a splendid Montale poem. A preoccupation with time, loss and an irretrievable past is evident, as is intelligent use of form, rhyme and structure.

A glance in the mirror at an ageing body initiates a flight of memory to the "awkward angular boy" returning from a fishing expedition in 'Brave Day'. Each of four stanzas represents a shift in the poem's narrative from shock and despair at the present to an idealised past, reminiscent of a Hovis advert, to a double-edged conclusion:

> Oh poisoned world,
> where bread was bread, and live frogs
> ten to the sovereign, for pike bait.

Morre's images hint and interact more than declare. Boy conscripts watching homebound trains and Hemingway staring hungrily into Paris bakery windows in 'Sometimes I dial' become fingers which "drift to the wound..." and segue into "Sometimes I dial the first digits of your number/ knowing your husband's in. Your nightdress/ hangs on the towel-rail". An unspoken narrative backgrounds itself in this well-paced poem and progresses from an attraction to a source of hurt (fingers to wound) to a more complex set of emotions stemming from a broken relationship. Morre may, like the mule in his poem 'Onager', have his "bum to the zeitgeist", but this collection deserves to outlive it.

Chris Andrews's second collection, *Lime Green Chair*, is tightly organised. The middle section contains philosophical vignettes, many of which span several pages. Sections 1 and 3 contain poems of two unrhymed stanzas, the first with thirteen lines and the second with eight – 'extended sonnets', if you like. These offer a complex system of fragmented ideas and images, a phrase often seeming to suggest the one following by tangential association more than any coherent linear argument, but Andrews exerts more control than that might initially suggest. His world is a multitude of sensations like a film in split screen, "mine to assemble in imagination/ from parts never meant to compose any whole // yet" ('Continuous Screening'). Fatalistic, the narrator hangs out washing while expecting rain and knowing his view on the world is never more than provisional, symbolised by the "indiscriminate rain that falls all over / wedding plans and military operations / branded for cable news, precision hairdos / and the rubble of what was whole this morning".

Durability and flotsam vie for attention and, if the themes are serious, a sharp wit is also at play. 'Far Call' takes place "in a place so advanced all the public phones / are falling forever into disrepair" and in 'Envoy' Andrews ushers his own poems into the world while asking "how many super-durable monuments / are settling on the windscreens of cars in Rome". This makes it easy to forgive occasional forays into self-indulgence, such as 'Late Extra', where an alienated man pounds the night streets with "patience"

> because it takes a long time
> to walk your momentum into the pavement
> so you become a weightless register:
>
> a cloth bag
> full of the wind of your own motion.

This sounds very 'poetic' but is getting all too full of its own wind. I felt some of those middle section poems were striving so hard for significance that they tipped into overblown solemnity. However, the bulk of this fine collection contains fresh, invigorating work that will make your head swim with, as MacNeice put it, "the drunkenness of things being various".

Rob A. Mackenzie's second collection, *The Good News*, was published by Salt in April 2013.

ℬ

Live Albums

ZOË SKOULDING

W.N. Herbert, *Omnesia (Remix)*, Bloodaxe, £9.95, ISBN 9781852249694;
W.N. Herbert, *Omnesia (Alternative Text)*,
Bloodaxe, £9.95, ISBN 9781852249625;
Simon Jarvis, *Eighteen Poems*, Eyewear Publishing, £12.99, ISBN 9781908998033;
Redell Olsen, *Punk Faun: A Bar Rock Pastel*, Subpress, $15, ISBN 9781930068568

Omnesia comprises two volumes, the *Alternative Text* and *Remix*, a project W.N. Herbert describes as "both punk experiment and prog system" – simultaneously improvised and orchestrated. Prog is certainly a presence, as in 'Dream Ironing', where the four sides of Tangerine

Dream's 1977 live double album *Encore* accompany the ironing of old T-shirts. If the performance is "still live", its context is changed by mid-life domesticity; the poem undercuts the illusion that "we're the recording, not the scratchy vinyl / or the performance, not the ageing ear". This double collection, two different books with one almost-identical sequence in common, reveals the impossibility of capturing a moment of live authenticity, but simultaneously revels in a liveness of its own as it riffs and improvises through flawed takes and mis-hearings, as is suggested by the title's portmanteau evocation of omniscience and amnesia.

Herbert's poetic strategy is not so much to "tell it slant" as to swivel adroitly into a universe of doubles where the North becomes a different 'Metanorth' in each collection, or where Donat, the obscure Welsh saint, "saw ahead / of his head a fried dough halo, a churro torus". Each of the off-beat narratives that drives the collection is "another" story, an improbable version of events that makes the likelier stories seem less so. 'A Myth of Scotland' creates an alternative colonial history in which Scotland was transformed by the dramatic success of the Darien Scheme, and includes a celebration of the resulting Highland llama: "O humpless camel, eel-neckit sheep, / brocht tae Scotia owre the Deep fae Darien tae nibble neeps". Such remixes of national narratives comment intriguingly on the devolving UK context, but Herbert's interest in translation extends world-wide. In 'Karakoram' an encounter in China with the late Iranian poet Emran Salahi is remembered:

> Emran and I swop the names of birds:
> parastu for sparrow, kabootar for dove,
> he thinks that magpie may be chelchela

However, a note under the poem points out that in fact "parastu" and "chelchela" both mean "swallow", while "kabootar" is "pigeon" – and both of these languages are foreign in the Chinese mountains where "the ink strokes // for seven falling-rising tones or eagles" offer further possibilities. As versions proliferate, Herbert's dramatisation of unreliability is generous in its refusal to erase other perspectives.

An interest in translation, particularly of Russian poetry, evokes a different set of musical relationships for Simon Jarvis, whose enigmatic poem 'After Pushkin' is short enough to quote in full:

> A bell sounds, and I drop the book.
> The line dries out upon my lips.

It floats before it fails and dips
below the reach of listening.
The sound comes from the parking strip.
My enemy, my tune, my fear,
who sees into me with a single look,
how did you know to find me here?

The apparent simplicity of its rhyming tetrameter sharpens the tension
between sound and music, particularly a verbal music that is only fleetingly,
half-consciously felt "below the reach of listening" in a landscape of eerie
dislocation, while the echo of "enemy" in "sees into me" reveals the tune of
lyric as inescapable. In 'Lessons and Carols', which describes the
transformation of things to gifts, music is equally coercive:

How they can sing, can wheedle and tick and can rhyme
winningly to us, as though all we lose for them were
well lost, and given us only to lose in this way.

The sense of entrapment becomes increasingly intense as the poem
progresses through eight thirteen-line stanzas, the objects taking on
disturbingly human qualities. In images such as "the telephone smooth as a
baby, the shallow recessed / hand-holds which welcome me into my family
car", the familial as well as the familiar are made strange in ways that reveal
capitalism's infiltration of even the most personal aspects of our lives. Music,
the siren-singing of consumer goods or the poem's own, is an unavoidable
force patterning thoughts and interactions – in 'Night Office', for example,
"Each bears his rhythm like an inner star: / each is walked though by some
one line of stress". The poems expose this mechanism at work, offering no
means of escape but instead expanding against its pressure, often through
sentences that traverse whole pages to create mythic geographies
encompassing Dantë, Milton, Wordsworth and Bunyan as well as the UK's
ring roads and motorways. While 'Persephone' offers a journey "Down to the
sugar vertex, down to the end of the line", into an underworld "where her
song is the limit invisibly sounding design", Jarvis's work significantly
extends the limits of song in contemporary poetry.

An altogether noisier approach emerges in Redell Olsen's *Punk Faun: A
Bar Rock Pastel*. The faun, half-human, half-goat, becomes a means not just
of exploring the fuzzy interface between humans and 'nature', but exploding
the opposition between the two, as in 'for songs at tongue', which announces:

"I give you the naturally made-up". This is a poetics of flamboyant rupture that clashes historical models, in this case the pastoral setting of the masque, with contemporary registers:

Come Queen of Muzak a blot

on enhanced contours Come
nail bar hands beat the ground
in a light Campari round this

plasma blister jollity in dance
of armoured personals of airy
shells of emergent fiery clouds

of scrambling net enhanced
chrones clad plastic face off
pixel caress in cabled nook

The element of performance that runs through the collection is most prominent in 'as performed in our own person', which imagines a series of actions to be presented in public places, for example:

in homage to the cupids in Domenichino's The Assumption of Mary Magdalen into Heaven, 1617-1621, I will ascend the escalator at Waterloo Station wearing a wing shaped ruff fashioned from today's newspaper.

Here, the details of everyday life – a railway station, a newspaper – form a stage set in which relations between background and foreground, and between artwork and viewer, are wittily configured. The ecological dimensions of Olsen's baroque folding of space and time are evident in "barriers at map", where the electronic tracking of deer in a landscape involves "passing through noise tuning specific / adjustments towards effects at present making / stag shift to become ones own musical performance". In this encounter between human and animal, who is acting and who is observing? If the difference between noise and "musical performance" lies in the kind of listening brought to a particular situation, *Punk Faun* makes these shifts in attention central to the poem – and to the noisy complexity of experiencing the world.

Zoë Skoulding is Senior Lecturer at Bangor University and Editor of *Poetry Wales*. Her collection, *The Museum of Disappearing Sands*, is due from Seren in October 2013.

THE GEOFFREY DEARMER PRIZE 2012

JUDGE: JANE DRAYCOTT

There were well over sixty poems eligible for the 2012 Geoffrey Dearmer Prize, all from strong emerging voices curated by a variety of different editors, which has made for an especially rich field from which to have to pick particular flowers. Of the many poems I read and returned to again and again, five left enduring imprints no matter how often I re-read them – imaginatively, musically, in terms of the authority and associative power with which they explored the worlds they dramatised. They were Nicholas Laughlin's complex and thought-provoking 'Reading History', Candy Neubert's delicately building, quietly explosive 'ways to leave', Richard Scott's sensuous, highly charged 'Maz', Ben Wilkinson's 'The Nightmare' with its compelling fusion of the visionary and the real, and finally Kayo Chingonyi's winning poems from 'calling a spade a spade'. Chingonyi's vision places an intimate, edgy sense of the individual experience – uncertain, intuitively resistant to easy-reach categorisations ("some words in this argot catch / in the throat, seemingly made for someone else") – dynamically and responsively in the pathway of historical developments in colour politics ("These days I can't watch a music video / online without you trolling in the comments / dressed to kill in your new age binary clothes"). His language is wonderfully searching, his imagery a series of small doors opening onto a whole house echoing with harmonic play and set with delicate rhythmic trip wires. Out of settings we can't fail to recognise ("dark means street / which means beast which means leave now for Benfleet"), 'calling a spade a spade' speaks with a highly distinctive voice. Other strong contenders were Sophie Clarke's 'Internet Dating', Sarah Howe's 'from A Certain Chinese Encyclopedia', Diriye Osman's 'Watering the Imagination', Kate Miller's 'Again (Reprise)', Rosie Shepperd's '"Don't take drugs, Allen, get married"' and Tom Warner's 'Wallets'.

The Geoffrey Dearmer Prize is awarded annually to the best *Poetry Review* poem written by a poet who doesn't yet have a full collection. It is funded through the generosity of the Dearmer family in honour of the poet Geoffrey Dearmer, who was a Poetry Society member.

Jane Draycott's most recent collection *Over* was shortlisted for the 2009 T.S. Eliot Prize. Her translation of the medieval dream-vision *Pearl* was published by Carcanet/ OxfordPoets in 2011.

Kayo Chingonyi
from calling a spade a spade

The N Word

You came back as rubber lips, pepper grains, blik
you're so black you're blik and how the word stuck to
our tongues eclipsing – or so we thought – the fear
that any moment anyone might notice
and we'd be deemed the wrong side of a night sky.
Lately you are a *pretty little lighty* who can
get dark because – even now – dark means street
which means beast which means leave now for Benfleet.
These days I can't watch a music video
online without you trolling in the comments
dressed to kill in your new age binary clothes.

The Cricket Test

Picture a cricket match, first week at upper
school, blacks versus whites, that slight hesitation
on choosing a side, and you're close to knowing
why I've been trying to master this language.
Raised as I was, some words in this argot catch
in the throat, seemingly made for someone else
(the sticking point from which all else is fixed).
We lost to a one-handed catch. After the match
our changing room was a shrine to apartheid.
When I crossed the threshold, Danny asked me why
I'd stand here when I could be there, with my kind.

The italicised phrases in 'The N Word' are borrowed from the song 'Get Dark' by Mz Bratt.

Both of the poems above were published in *Poetry Review*, 102:4, Winter 2012, guest-edited by Bernardine Evaristo. A new poem, 'The Room', is published overleaf.

The Room

when you sample you're not just picking up that sound,
you're picking up the room it was recorded in
                                                    – Oddisee

For the purist, hung up on tracing a drum break
to its source, acquired in the few moments grace

before the store-clerk, thin voiced, announces closing time
it's not just the drummer's slack grip, how the hook line

swings in the session singer's interpretation,
or the engineer's too-loud approximation

of the MacGyver theme tune, it's that hiss, the room
fetching itself from itself in hiccups and spools.

Though there's a knack in telling a-side, from remix,
from test press that never saw the light of day

mere completists never learn a good song's secret;
air displaced in that room – the breath of acetate.

Kayo Chingonyi was born in Zambia in 1987, moving to the UK in 1993. He holds a BA in English Literature from the University of Sheffield, an MA in Creative Writing from Royal Holloway, University of London, and works as a writer, events producer and creative writing tutor.

His poems have been published in a range of magazines and anthologies including *Poetry Review, Magma, Wasafiri, The Best British Poetry 2011* (Salt Publishing, 2011), *The Salt Book of Younger Poets* (Salt Publishing, 2011), *Out Of Bounds* (Bloodaxe, 2012), *The World Record* (Bloodaxe, 2012), and in a debut pamphlet entitled *Some Bright Elegance* (Salt Publishing, 2012).

Kayo has also been invited to read from his work at venues and events across the UK and internationally. In 2012 he represented Zambia at Poetry Parnassus, a festival of world poets staged by the Southbank Centre as part of the London 2012 Festival. He was recently shortlisted for the inaugural Brunel University African Poetry Prize.

CONTRIBUTORS

Antonella Anedda has published five books of poetry, most recently *Salva con nome* (Save As) which won the Viareggio Prize for Poetry. **Tara Bergin**'s debut collection *This is Yarrow* is due from Carcanet in July. **Volker Braun** is the author of plays, novels and essays, as well as ten volumes of poetry. His many prizes include the Georg-Büchner-Preis in 2000. **John Clegg**'s first collection, *Antler*, was published by Salt in 2012. **Peter Cole**'s fourth collection, *The Invention of Influence*, is published next year in the US by New Directions. **Claire Crowther** has published two collections of poetry and three pamphlets, the most recent of which is *Incense*. **Antony Dunn** has published three collections of poetry, most recently *Bugs* (Carcanet OxfordPoets, 2009). **Helen Farish** won the Forward Prize for Best First Collection for *Intimates* (2005); in 2012 she published *Nocturnes at Nohant*. **Charles Mundye** lectures in English at the University of Hull, and is the editor of *Keidrych Rhys, The Van Pool: Collected Poems* for Seren (2012). **Jennie Feldman**'s new collection *Swift* was published by Anvil Press last year. **Valeria Ferraro**'s most recent books are *wasurenamu* and *Zoology*. **Donald Gardner** is a poet and literary translator who lives in Amsterdam. **Richard Gwyn**'s most recent books are *The Vagabond's Breakfast* (2011), a memoir, which won a Wales Book of the Year award, and *A Complicated Mammal: Selected Poems of Joaquín O. Giannuzzi* (2012). **Stefan Hertmans** is a major figure in contemporary Flemish literature. Recent titles include *De val van vrije dagen* (*The Free Fall of Days*, 2010) and *De mobilisatie van Arcadia* (2011). His novel, *War and Turpentine* will be published in September. Born in Colorado, **Julith Jedamus**'s first collection, *The Swerve*, was published by Carcanet in 2012; she is currently working on a book of translations of Federico García Lorca. **Carolyn Jess-Cooke**'s debut poetry collection *INROADS* received a number of awards, including a Northern Promise Award. **Dore Kiesselbach**'s collection, *Salt Pier*, containing work selected by Jackie Kay for the Bridport Prize, won a noted American first-book contest. **Gregory Leadbetter**'s pamphlet *The Body in the Well* appeared in 2007, and his book *Coleridge and the Daemonic Imagination* won the CCUE Book Prize 2012. **Karen Leeder** is Professor of Modern German Literature at the University of Oxford. Her translation of Evelyn Schlag's *Selected Poems* (Carcanet, 2004) won the Schlegel-Tieck Prize. She is working on Volker Braun's *Selected Poems* with the poet David Constantine. **Gabriel Levin** is the author of four collections, most recently *To These Dark Steps* (Anvil, 2012) and a collection of essays, *The Dune's Twisted Edge: Journeys in the Levant* (The University of Chicago Press, 2013). **Jamie McKendrick**'s most recent book of poems is *Out There*, and his translation of Antonella Anedda's poems, *Archipelago*, is due next year from Bloodaxe. **Philip Morre**'s latest collection is *The Sadness of Animals* (San Marco Press, 2012). **D. Nurkse** is the author of ten books of poetry. CB Editions is publishing the UK edition of his most recent collection, *A Night in Brooklyn*. **Dan O'Brien** is a poet and playwright in Los Angeles. His play *The Body of an American* won the inaugural Edward M. Kennedy Prize for Drama. **Mario Petrucci** has recently completed *i tulips*, his 1111-strong Anglo-American sequence from which *the waltz in my blood* (Waterloo, 2011) and *anima* (Nine Arches Press, 2013) are excerpts. **Rodney Pybus**'s seventh collection, *Darkness Inside Out*, was published at the end of last year (Northern House/Carcanet Press). **John Redmond** teaches Creative Writing at the University of Liverpool. His most recent book is *Poetry and Privacy* (Seren). **Stephen Romer**'s recent translations from the French include Yves Bonnefoy's *The Arrière-pays* (Seagull, 2012) and *French Decadent Tales* (Oxford World's Classics, 2013). **Kathryn Simmonds**'s second collection, *The Visitations*, is published by Seren in October. **Jean Sprackland**'s fourth collection, *Sleeping Keys*, will be published by Cape in September. **A.E. Stallings** is an American poet who lives in Athens. Her most recent collection is *Olives*. **Jimmy Symonds** is freelance photographic artist, writer and educator. **Helen Tookey**'s first full-length collection, *Missel-Child*, is forthcoming from Carcanet in January 2014. **David Wheatley** is the author of *Flowering Skullcap* (Wurm Press, 2012). **Sam Willetts** is currently working on a collection of poems to follow his 2010 debut *New Light For The Old Dark* (Cape Poetry). **William Wootten**'s poems have appeared in magazines including *The Rialto*, *The Spectator* and *The Times Literary Supplement*. **Jordan A. Yamaji Smith** is Assistant Professor of Comparative World Literature & Classics at California State University Long Beach, and has also translated works from Nomura Kiwao, Takayuki Suzuki, Alberto Fuguet, and Fernando Iwasaki.